CALLED TO
LEAD

CALLED TO
LEAD

**OVERCOMING THE CHALLENGES OF MINISTRY
IN A MALE-DOMINATED SPACE AS A WOMAN OF FAITH**

DR. MADELENE F. BEARD

Printed in the United States of America

Called to Lead: Overcoming the Challenges of Ministry in a Male-Dominated Space as a Woman of Faith by Dr. Madelene F. Beard

ISBN: Paperback - 979-8-9917761-1-0

Hardcover - 979-8-9917761-4-1

Published by: Tucker Publishing House, LLC

11000 W. McNichols Rd, Suite 323, Detroit, MI 48221

Printed in the United States of America

First Printing, December 2024

Cover Design: Janika (TPH, LLC)

For permissions requests or inquiries, please contact Tucker Publishing House, LLC at the address above.

Disclaimer: This book is designed to provide information for personal growth and encouragement. It is sold with the understanding that the author and publisher are not engaged in rendering legal, psychological, or other professional services.

TABLE OF CONTENTS

DEDICATION

This book is dedicated to all the women who have heard the "call" but are reluctant to answer because of the adversity in the atmosphere.

My dear late mother, Evelyn Beatrice, who gave birth to me, loved me and supported my ministry until she was no longer able.

My late father, Alfred Tennyson, believed in the power of prayer.

The Galatians United Church of Christ Family.

Deborah's Women In Ministry, Inc., of Greater Hampton Roads.

The late Rev. Martha E. Reid paved the way for me to become pastor of Galatians.

My late pastor, Rev. George A. Speight, Sr., and my home church, Mineral Spring Baptist Church. (MSBC)

To the late Mrs. Ernestine T. Langston. She was responsible for my joining MSBC with her and her family. Mrs. Langston was the epitome of mother-hood and a great mentor in my Christian journey. She would later be the person who recommended me for my first professional job. She also encouraged me as I advanced in my career.

Mrs. Martha S. Gordon strongly believed that God was calling me to ministry. She was responsible for booking my first speaking engagement outside the church, a prayer breakfast. Mrs. Gordon was full of encouragement.

**Download my free prayer eBook to
encourage you in life and ministry.**

FOREWORD

〰〰〰〰〰〰

Inviting!! Captivating!! These are words that I use to describe the spirit and action that move from cover to cover in this book, **Called to Lead.** Dr. Madelene F. Beard launches us into deep waters to discuss how women in ministry should maneuver in a male-dominated space. While Dr. Beard has overcome many trials and obstacles, she possesses the strength and fortitude to press forward as a woman minister.

Walk with me as I paint a picture of **Called to Lead's** impact on my life.

It all began over 50 years ago, with me teaching one of Dr. Beard's children, meeting her family, and then becoming a part of her church ministry—serving as an Associate Minister at Galatians UCC in Suffolk, VA.

In 2012, I joined "Deborah's Women In Ministry, Inc. of Greater Hampton Roads" (DWIM), where Dr. Madelene is our founder, president, and CEO. She established this organization to mentor women in ministry and those aspiring to the ministry. Our mission is to 'affirm, equip, and educate women in ministry' following Deborah's lead in Judges 4: 4-5.

Now, speaking from my perspective as 1st Vice President of DWIM, I am afforded the opportunity to experience the methodology that Dr. Madelene uses to help individuals discern what God has called them to do in ministry.

This book, **Called to Lead,** *uncovers* aspects of her journey that exemplify her strength in dealing with being a woman in a male-dominated space.

As DWIM members, we look, listen, and learn. Dr. Madelene's transparency about her struggles, trials, and triumphs encourages us to put aside our reservations and speak out about the same types of situations.

Under Dr. Madelene's leadership, she has taught us how to overcome these challenges of ministry in a male-dominated space. She maps out a plan of activities that mixes conferences with social gatherings and study sessions with prayer vigils. Each entity is an opportunity that stresses the importance of women taking an assertive posture and finding their way forward in a male-dominated space.

At each DWIM meeting, time is designated for "business." Then, there is time set aside for us to gather around the table, open our Bibles and our hearts, and strategize how to break through the obstacles we face within the ministry as women.

Dr. Madelene seizes every opportunity to make sure that we understand what we need to do to 'stand firm' in our faith when we are attacked on every side. With these imperatives in mind, we can move forward and share what we know that works with all of God's children.

Let me convey to you Dr. Madelene's stance on the matter: "We are neither uncertain or hesitant to speak forcefully about what we have endured. We're not 'male-bashing'. We put situations and circumstances into a sifter, shake them down, pour them out, weigh our options, and take the next step towards living life as God would have us to do."

Dr. Beard's influence extends to the church, Galatians UCC, Suffolk, VA. She was confident that God had a plan for her life, and that plan gave her a firm foundation—laid by her faith—in His excellent Word. She was called, anointed, and appointed by God. She gained the power to overcome obstacles, excel in any challenge, and exceed any expectations. Her leadership and tutelage for over 38 years have emboldened the church to move forward with community service that brings glory to God.

Because of Dr. Madelene's heart, yoked with her leadership and perseverance, church members willingly and joyfully have worked to develop new ministries within the church, have stepped up to be "lay leaders" within the local church and the wider church, and have donated 'anything and everything' needed to make Galatians what it is today. Galatians is a 'thriving' church.

Another one of her 'marks of distinction' is her preaching. When she preaches, she elevates your mind and touches your heart using illustrations that capture your attention and keep you focused on the Word of God. Dr. Madelene makes it relevant, keeps it real, and brings it down to earth. Make no mistake, she's got the theological depth, exegetical breath, and homiletical height that defy the contents of any ordinary sermon. What's even better, she practices what she preaches. She lives a life that exemplifies the walk of a solid Christian leader.

Dr. Madelene labors for the Lord because He is the center of her life. She gives freely of her time – her talents – and her treasure to ensure that whatever God's people need is what they get. Proverbs 31:31 attests to it: "—the works of her hands" – she is "productive."

Because of her productivity, Dr. Beard received the "Servant Leader of the Year" award from the Black Girl Magic Alliance. This Alliance is a platform on which women of color share their stories about the transformative power of God.

As Tod Bolsinger calls it, "Tempered resilience" is where Dr. Madelene unpacks the miracles in her life that make her successful in the secular world and ministry.

So, take the journey with me in reading this book, **Called to Lead,** and experience the paradigm shift that uncovers what unwavering faith and perseverance have done in Dr. Beard's life. I promise you – an unforgettable adventure!! Following her lead can also help you overcome the challenges in ministry in a male-dominated space.

Thank you, Dr. Madelene, for asking me to write the foreword to your book. Your superb exposition challenges us to take the next step in doing what God has called us to do. (Philippians 4: 13, NIV)

Rev. Ann Watson Hill, Ph.D.
1st Vice President
Deborah's Women In Ministry, Inc. of Greater Hampton Roads

Endorsement from a Classmate:
Dr. Veronica R. Coleman

I am honored to endorse this timely and necessary book, *Called to Lead: Overcoming the Challenges of Ministry in a Male-Dominated Space as a Woman of Faith.* The author, Rev. Dr. Madelene Beard, has served the church faithfully for over forty years, standing as a powerful testimony to God's sustaining grace and strength in the face of many trials. I had the privilege of walking alongside her during our time at the Samuel DeWitt Proctor School of Theology at Virginia Union University, where we both embarked on a journey to be equipped for our divine call to ministry. Her journey, and indeed her calling, speaks to the essence of this book—a book written for women who are called but who may feel unsure, overlooked, or even discouraged as they navigate ministry in spaces that weren't designed with them in mind.

For too long, our sisters in faith have struggled to find their place in a landscape dominated by male leadership. As the first woman licensed to preach the gospel in my own church, I intimately understand the trials and tribulations that come with answering God's call in spaces that were not designed for us.

Madelene Beard's book serves as the mentor many of us longed for but never had.

As I reflect on my own 25-year journey in ministry, I am struck by how much easier the path might have been with a resource like **Called to Lead** at my disposal. This book fills that void by providing a roadmap for those who feel called to lead but may be unsure of how to navigate the complexities of the journey. It offers practical advice, words of encouragement, and a deep understanding of the spiritual and emotional demands of ministry.

Whether you are just beginning your journey or have been serving the church for many years, **Called to Lead** will provide you with the tools and support you need to overcome obstacles, build your confidence, and fulfill your divine purpose. It is a book that will inspire, empower, and equip you to lead with courage, compassion, and faith.

To my sisters in Christ who have felt the weight of doubt or the sting of rejection in your ministerial journey, I say: Take heart! **Called to Lead** is here to remind you that you are not alone, that your voice matters, and that your leadership is not just welcome but essential to the flourishing of God's kingdom on earth.

As you read these pages, may you find the courage to walk boldly in your calling, knowing that you are not alone and that the God who called you is faithful to carry you through.

May this book serve as a source of strength, a fount of wisdom, and a catalyst for change in our churches and communities. Let us heed Dr. Madelene's call and step boldly into the fullness of our divine purpose, knowing that we stand on the shoulders of those who came before us and pave the way for those who will follow.

In the spirit of Sojourner Truth, Jarena Lee, and all the powerful women who dared to preach when others said they couldn't – let us rise, let us lead, and let us transform the church with the unique gifts God has given us.

Dr. Veronica R. Coleman, Senior Pastor
New Jerusalem Ministries

INTRODUCTION

Throughout my journey, I have met many women in need of encouragement and direction in ministry. Some of them didn't even know where to begin, which often leads to confusion, frustration, and self-doubt.

I am writing this manual for women clergy. To those who have received authorized ministry—whether ordained or licensed—as well as laypersons who lead in their churches. It is also for students in seminary or specialized training programs, and for women who aspire to the ministry but have not yet discerned their calling.

This book is intended to serve as a guide for women who feel called to ministry but are unsure of where to start. I want to help you. The first step in your journey is self-examination—you must know who you are and to whom you belong. Having a clear understanding of yourself, your spirituality, and your beliefs about God's calling is crucial in discerning your ministry path.

Second, it's valuable to look at the experiences of other clergy members and compare your call story with theirs. However, be mindful that your call story doesn't need to mirror someone else's. God calls each of us in unique ways, using different images and experiences. Third, remember that God's call may lead you to forms of ministry you hadn't anticipated. In this book, I will share both embarrassing and painful moments as well as triumphant ones—moments that made the challenges worthwhile as I pressed toward the higher calling.

It's important to note that negative experiences in ministry are not the end of the journey. They do not mean that God hasn't called you or that ministry isn't for you. I've witnessed how these hardships often become stepping stones, guiding you to new levels in ministry under the leadership of the Holy Spirit. Women who feel called to ministry and are ready to move forward will find this book to be a source of strength and guidance as they grow in their calling. I accepted the call to ministry in the mid-1980s, determined to do what I believed God had called me to do. However, I was always concerned about how my husband would react to the news. Although he was a man of faith, he had once shared a story about a young woman he had liked—until she became an evangelist. That memory made me nervous about telling him I felt called to the ministry.

At that time, female clergy were not widely accepted in ministry or church leadership, and they still aren't in some religious traditions today.

When I finally told my husband about my calling, I was relieved by his response. He said, "I already knew God had a calling on your life. I was just wondering when you'd share it with me." After a long conversation, he encouraged me to talk to our pastor. I felt nervous once again, but I made an appointment.

When I explained to my pastor that God had called me to ministry, he smiled and said, "I know. I've been waiting for you to come to me." His response amazed me. I realized that both my husband and my pastor had already seen the anointing in my life. After acknowledging my call, I preached my initial sermon on Sunday, September 30, 1984. The Holy Spirit moved powerfully that day, and one year later, my pastor and the church ordained me.

Under my pastor's guidance, I enrolled in a two-year religious program. During that time, I continued my ministry at my home church, preaching, visiting the sick, teaching Sunday school, alternating Bible study with the pastor, and serving on the Missionary Circle. I also accepted preaching assignments at other churches, with my pastor's approval.

My spiritual and academic growth accelerated as I remained humbled and determined to succeed in ministry. With the support of my pastor, church, family, professors and my beloved husband I grew stronger in my calling.

In 1987, Galatians United Church of Christ called me to serve as their pastor. To receive full endorsement as an authorized clergy member, the United Church of Christ required me to graduate from an ATS-accredited seminary. After completing my studies at the Samuel DeWitt Proctor School of Theology, I was ordained for the second time, this time by both the Eastern Virginia Association of the United Church of Christ and Galatians.

I have now served the church faithfully for 38 years. It has been a blessing and an honor to serve both the congregation and the surrounding community. When I first took the helm, the church was grieving the loss of its previous pastor. It had been struggling to find a sense of normalcy. I knew the task ahead of me was daunting, but I also knew that God would guide me.

I prayed continually, asking God for strength to rebuild His kingdom on earth. Through prayer and perseverance, I led the congregation in projects that revitalized the church and moved us forward in our mission. This unique calling has been a powerful blessing. I am grateful for the opportunity to serve and lead.

When I first began, I encountered people who told me, "You don't look like a minister." At first, I didn't think much of it, but over time I realized they were implying that, as a woman, I didn't belong in the ministry. Some would ask, "Are you sure God called you to ministry?" Or they comment on my appearance, saying things like, "You're too pretty to be a minister." In response, I tried dressing more conservatively and wearing less makeup. But no matter how I presented myself, the comments persisted. People assumed my husband was a pastor and that I'd become a minister through him. The cynics couldn't accept that God had called me, a woman, to serve Him.

I want to encourage women clergy to think assertively and confidently, just like their male counterparts. When a woman is confident in herself and relies on God's guidance, she can move mountains.

This manual is written to encourage, equip, and educate women who feel called to ministry, no matter what area of ministry they pursue. I speak this directly to you: Thank you for investing in yourself, and courageously moving forward in your calling.

Sincerely,
Reverend Dr. Madelene F. Beard

A Prayer for Courage and Wisdom

Dear God, the Creator and Sustainer of life, I adore and praise You for who You are and for the life You have blessed me with. Through struggles, hurts, and rejections, You have seen me through. Thank You, God, for sending Your only begotten Son, Jesus Christ, so that we may have the right to eternal life. Thank You for Your unconditional love, grace, and mercy. I stand in awe of Your creation and am humbled that You have called me to serve as a pastor, wife, mother, and a leader in the faith community. I am deeply grateful for the family, friends, and resources You have placed in my life. I am honored to be a trailblazer, a role model, and a source of encouragement for other women called to ministry. When hope seems lost, remind us to encourage ourselves, as David did, in the Lord our God (1 Samuel 30:6). May my experiences, wounds, doubts, and triumphs—empower the beautiful and gifted women discerning Your call to ministry. In the name of the Father, the Son, and the Holy Spirit, I pray, Amen.

CHAPTER 1

JUST BEING FEMALE CAUSES AN UPROAR

*"Let your women keep silence in the churches: for
it is not permitted unto them to speak; but they are
commanded to be under obedience,
as also saith the law"*
–1 Corinthians 14: 34 (KJV).

When God created women, He made them fearfully and wonderfully, expressing to them their works are wonderful as well (Psalm 139:14-NIV). We often think about our birthrights, our looks, and to whom we were born. When God made a woman, He made a human being filled with compassion, tenderness, love, mercy, creativity, nurturing, and a diligent worker. As I see it, she bears the attributes of Christ.

Proverbs 31:10 (KJV) describes the woman as one who is virtuous. The question is asked, "Who can find a virtuous woman? For her price is far above rubies?" According to Webster's New World College Virtuous means "having or being characterized by moral virtue; righteous."

The proverbial woman supports and is concerned about her husband and family. She is a doer and an industrious worker. She provides for the needy and participates in a plethora of activities to provide for her family and the community. A virtuous woman can serve the whole gamut of things to accomplish God's mission on earth. Thus, when God made women, he made a remarkable, gifted, and talented human being.

Given a woman's giftedness and virtues, when she enters a room, she causes an uproar because she has so much to offer God's people.

My maternal grandmother was a proverbial woman. She prayed constantly and enjoyed playing the organ early in the morning. I find myself emulating my grandmother. When I do my devotions in the morning, I usually end with playing a hymn on the piano. I celebrate my maternal grandmother because, in a sense, she was my first minister—my spiritual role model. She taught me the Lord's Prayer and the 23rd Psalms. She encouraged me to learn Bible verses by writing them on brown paper and putting them under my pillow at night. She would always say, "You will remember the Lord's word by doing that."

Navigating Stereotypes and Cultural Expectations

A sizable percentage of women may have a colossal amount of experience in ministry and possess a wide range of academic degrees. However, unfortunately, they still face prejudice and discrimination in the 21st-century church.

We still must navigate through the many stereotypical experiences in ministry. Here are four examples of biases that still exist today, and we must deal with them. First, in certain faith traditions, a female clergy is made an evangelist or minister in her church instead of some form of authorized ministry. Authorized ministry means that the person is ordained to do ministry. Unless she is kin to the pastoral leadership, she will most likely be a first-class waitress to the participants in the pulpit, not an armor bearer, but a waitress or usher. Of course, it depends on how the church is set up from the top down. Second, it is typical for male clergy to be acknowledged by their titles. On the other hand, women clergy are subject not to be mentioned or are often referred to as "sisters," even when she is degreed. Many male clergy are not academically prepared, but they still get highly recognized over the well-educated female clergy. Third, when the male clergy gather, they will greet and shake the hands of their contemporaries. However, women are often left unrecognized and alone on the sideline unless someone has a particular interest or concern in them.

It seems to me that the cultural norms in some of our established black communities and black churches are not supportive of the female clergy for the most part. As I see it, the black church and community basically practice and are in concert with the same cultural ideals because we are products of our environment.

The powers that be in the black church still prefer to have male ministers and pastors do revivals. Due to today's pressures from women in leadership, the planners will ask at least one female clergy member to do a night's revival—not every night, just one night. Male evangelists will cover the remaining nights.

As the cultural norm dictates, the manna days—Holy Week and Passion Week services all have male clergy delivering the messages. There is always an excuse, but it's so evident that it's the "good old-boy" system. Even males dominate the dais. When asked, "Why?" There are still excuses prevailing.

Based on my experience, it's not necessarily the older generation that doesn't believe that women can be called to ministry. Some of the younger generations—young men and women-- can be just as prejudiced.

Consequently, many young people resist the cultural force and break through traditional barriers by moving away from their childhood communities. Once relocated, they will be exposed to new concepts that encourage new cognitive awareness. So, they begin to look at life differently, enabling them to think independently.

A case in point is a family or a church steeped in tradition and cultural norms that will apply and execute those ideals and precepts, whether in favor of women in leadership or not.

Some mainline denominations have embraced and approved women in ministry to join the church leadership. Various churches and denominations have not fully approved equality for the female clergy. I believe these stereotypes will continue unless the national church and local church pastors teach and promote women clergy in leadership. There will be little growth in the mindset of the faith communities.

Embracing Your Identity as a Woman of God

I embraced my identity as a woman of God long before I accepted the call to ministry. My mother, grandmothers, and teachers were excellent role models to emulate as I developed into adulthood. At an early age, they taught me to live by God's Word, keep his commandments, pray, be the best I could in life, and always give God my best service.

To identify as a woman of God, I pride myself on being a virtuous daughter, granddaughter, wife, mother, grandmother, sister, auntie, friend, church member, employee, and pastor. In everything that I do, I always try to please God and represent His goodness.

As a female minister, I carry myself well. I never act masculine. I always maintain my femininity. The ladies in my family and home church were the epitome of womanhood. Therefore, I was socialized to be a God-fearing, graceful, and well-posed lady of God.

As I dwelt with the call of God in my life, I discovered that it was humbling and an honor to be a woman of God. It was overwhelming that God chose me to be a servant leader.

As the second oldest child in my family unit, I was always the one who took the lead in caring for my younger siblings. At eight, I taught them to love each other, be well-behaved, and kept them fed and clean while my parents worked. Around 8:30 every night, I set up a cardboard box, my pulpit, to teach and preach to them. The box was bigger than I was. Sometimes, they would run and hide; other times, they would listen patiently to what I had to say. I also taught them to pray the Lord's Prayer, as my grandmother had taught me. I also helped my parents take care of various aspects of their business.

My mother relocated to another state to advance her career. There, we bonded with the Freemans, who were friends of our family. They became like our parents. The Freemans assumed my Grandma's teaching role. Looking back, it was as if they saw the same gifts and talents in me. They continued teaching and grooming us both. I was the one they tried to make a little missionary. I always read scriptures, poems, and recitations for various church events. The Freemans were a godsend to me and my sister Shirley, who was much younger than I.

As I matured, I could see God's purpose for my life. Of course, I never envisioned, at that time, that I would become a pastor. God's unique purpose for me was to be a leader in my family unit, the church, and the community.

I have had vast experiences in the ministry, which were both unpleasant, good, and celebratory. Even the unpleasant ones humbled me and prepared me for a lifetime of ministry with humankind.

About a month after I preached my initial sermon, an elderly lady who belonged to one of the churches in the community approached me after a service one Sunday afternoon with a hurtful question. She said, "What are you trying to prove by entering the ministry? You need to find yourself something else to do." I was hurt because she was one of the ladies I admired and respected with all my heart. I smiled at her and said, "I am not trying to prove anything to anybody because God has called me into the ministry." I cried all the way home that day. Not that I doubted myself and my calling, but this experience was thought-provoking. I often reflected on it and wondered why the lady needed to express her negative thoughts to me.

I have attended funerals where I was asked to pray or read scripture, and then 5-8 minutes later, one of the brethren showed up, and the Officiant would take the assignment from me and give it to the male minister that arrived. In retrospect, there was no previous commitment between the two ministers.

On the contrary, God has blessed me with one of the most positive ministry experiences a pastor would want. He called me to a church that was in decline, but to God be the glory, I was able to help save the church from dying even when the conference leaders thought that it might not survive.

Also, I founded an organization for women in ministry that has provided them with a safe place to share their frustrations, concerns, aspirations, and celebrations in life. I am thankful that God has permitted me to be a guiding light for them. God is worthy to be praised!

Chapter Summary:

- Women's intrinsic value and divine purpose should be celebrated and recognized.

- Despite facing stereotypes and cultural biases, women in ministry can navigate these challenges and embrace their God-given identity.

- Women can find strength and inspiration in their roles, supported by faith, prayer, and positive role models.

- Creating supportive communities and breaking traditional barriers can foster greater equality and recognition for women in ministry.

Self-Reflection:

1. Which scripture describes the woman as a proverbial woman? Reference the scripture, and list five traits of a virtuous woman.

   _____

   _____

   _____

   _____

   _____

2. Do you believe that "being a female in ministry" causes an uproar? If you do, explain. If not, cite your reason.

   _____

   _____

   _____

   _____

   _____

3. If you are in the ministry or aspiring to be in ministry, have you had to navigate stereotypes? List at least two experiences that you had to navigate through.

   _____

   _____

   _____

   _____

   _____

4. Describe how you have embraced your identity as a Woman of God.

_____

_____

_____

_____

_____

CHAPTER 2

STOP THE JEALOUSY – I CAN FEEL IT COMING FROM YOU

"To another the working of miracles, to another prophecy, to another discerning of spirits..."
—*1 Corinthians 12: 10 (NKJV).*

Have you ever entered a relationship, an organization, a church, or a work community and were made to feel as comfortable as possible? The people who welcomed and embraced you expressed love and appreciation for you. From their mouths came expressions like: "You are the best," "Where have you been all this time?" You are just who I needed," "I will always love and respect you." By the way, I love the expression (being cynical): "I love you, and there's nothing you can do about it." The latter phrase sounds great, but does it come from the heart?

Then, just as you are comfortable and feeling all warm and fuzzy with your current situation, you realize something has gone awry. You discern an ill spirit in the atmosphere that is causing you some angst. Let's pause right here! Some people forget that God has given others the spirit of discernment. What does the term discernment mean? Webster's New World College Dictionary defines discernment as "the power of discerning, keen perception, judgment or insight." I Corinthians 12:10 supports the explanation because the text states, "to another discerning of spirits." This means you may be able to discern foreign spirits and false doctrines as well. This is a spiritual gift that God gives us to help guide and protect us through life's journey.

I have experienced jealousy all too many times from women who vowed to be my best "sister friend" – I thought they were genuine, spiritually mature, and wholesome. Once my God-given discernment kicked in, I would think, "Hear we go again; I can't believe this person so endeared to me is jealous of my God-given personality and outgoing ways." It is gut-wrenching, frightening, heartbreaking, and hurtful. It turns asunder all the good that you thought that person was to you, which, on the other hand, may cause you not to trust people. Jealousy from a sister or any person you've trusted with all your heart can be disappointing and possibly devastating for the remainder of your life.

Over the years, I have accomplished many things—thanks to God. My successes came with a dichotomy of jealousy and competition. We can overcome the agony once we recognize and realize that the jealousy a "sister-friend" projects is not about you. It's important to note that jealousy can reflect how you feel about yourself.

Sadly, competition is present in the ministry ranks as well, period. However, I hate to think that competition prevails amongst our dear clergy sisters as often as it does.

If you aren't doing anything in life, some people seem to love you, and you become their favorite person to talk to and be in your presence. But don't dare be about improving your life—setting personal goals and accomplishing the same. Then you find out who your friends are. Some of the high achievers want to keep you down.

Our Christian responsibility is cultivating a spirit of unity and support for female clergy in the ministry. Someone must be a Christ-like role model to encourage unity and support others trying to move forward.

When a lady clergyperson comes to me for advice and instruction, I happily and prayerfully try to assist and guide her spiritually and earnestly. I will refer her to a reliable or professional source if I do not have the knowledge or expertise to help her. I do not take the attitude that I have mine; she has hers to get. That type of attitude is not of God.

Celebrating each other's successes is not only important but healthy for our mental wellbeing. I recall when I became pastor of my church, I was concerned about how I would "fit" with the congregation and help them to grow. I also wanted to renovate the building, among many other things. Given those interests and concerns, I was HAPPY to become a new pastor because I felt that was the assignment that God called me to do. Consequently, not everyone shared my joy. I discerned that some people were sincerely happy for me, while others had no comments at all. BUT there were others—women and men— who made negative expressions every time they were in my presence. The naysayers would make comments like, "Had the church been a big church, they wouldn't have called a woman in the first place." Another would say, "Oh, you'll never make it here, it's too much work to be done." Yet, another expressed that I was a female and too young to take on a challenge like that." In a nutshell, a few of them were people who tried pastoring [supposedly friends of mine], but it didn't work out for them. I felt a spirit of jealousy every time I saw them. The question would come: "Are you still at that little church in the woods?" Smiles always covered my face. I would say, "Yes, I'm still there—thank God for his favor." I refused to let them erase the colors from my rainbow.

Conversely, there were several who thought I was a good visionary, had smarts, and excellent ideas for ministry. But seemingly, the more I did, the more the naysayers minimized my successes. I could never improve the church fast enough. Or my parishioners didn't have enough initiative to move forward. Their negative comments and actions would crush my spirit only for a minute. Therefore, I wouldn't let them get the best of me. Why? Because I trusted God with all my heart and soul, and I knew that He didn't bring me this far to leave me. Whenever I needed God, He was always nearby.

Earlier in this writing, I reflected on several experiences regarding jealousy but there are two others that I wish to share with my readers because I feel this will help you navigate through jealousy.

During my younger and more attractive years, I met jealous spirits in the churches and other places I frequented. Sometimes being attractive and young can be a double-edged sword. I have often thought on this scripture, "...I am fearfully and wonderfully made..." (Psalm 139:14). The gentlemen in most of the churches that I supplied or did special occasion preaching were always cordial and respectful. After I finished preaching, a couple of men would assist me down from the platform. This continued until their wives became jealous. I was informed that their wives said something to them about coming to greet me after preaching because one by one, the men scattered and stopped coming to assist me. During those days my husband's career kept him traveling, so he was absent a great deal of the time.

First, it's not always easy to navigate through jealousy because you are still a human being with feelings and emotions of your own. I found that a strong prayer life, reading and meditating on God's Word, and making use of other spiritual groups, helped me stay encouraged. The way I see it, if you don't keep yourself spiritually strong, you will succumb to depression or just simply give up on what God has called you to do. To dispel any presuppositions, that I may have been interested in the gentlemen. One Sunday morning, I made a statement letting the congregation know that I was very much married to my wonderful husband and not interested in their husbands, sons, brothers, uncles, etc. The expressions on their faces were amusing to say the least. In retrospect, I prayed asking God for direction concerning this matter. After that little speech, the gentlemen eventually started returning to assist me. It seems that God always prepared me with what to say and how to conduct myself—all at the right time—God's timing.

Lastly, God made it possible for me to become a contributing author to "Words of Wisdom for the Heart and Soul" Volume III, compiled by Visionary Cathy Staton. I was filled with such joy and happiness when the book was published. In sharing about my book, I would often say that I was an author, but a few friends have corrected me and said, "You just added to somebody else's book. I have written my own books—I wrote 7 books already." I told them that was not a problem for me, but I do plan to write other books in the future. I discerned a hint of jealousy along with minimizing my efforts of writing and authorship. My reply to the individuals, "That's nice, but I will always remain grateful to God for allowing me to be a part of a literary group." In short, I would have expected my friends to rejoice with me since I was so happy. So, as we experience jealousy, we must prepare ourselves to navigate through them in positive ways.

Chapter Summary:

- Recognizing and Addressing Jealousy: Recognize jealousy as a reflection of others' insecurities rather than a personal failing.

  Stay grounded in faith, prayer, and positive communication to navigate through jealousy.

- Encouraging Unity: Promote a spirit of unity and support, especially among female clergy, to counteract jealousy and competition.

  Celebrate each other's successes and maintain a positive outlook to foster a healthy, supportive community.

Self-Reflection:

1. Have you ever experienced jealousy? If so, write a short narrative of your experience. Explain how it made you feel at the time and whether you overcame the hurt or anguish.

_____

_____

_____

_____

_____

_____

_____

_____

2. Using at least three different biblical translations, read the following scriptures that mention discernment of the spirit: I Corinthians 12:10 and Hebrews 5:14. Explain how these scriptures have helped you to understand God-given discernments.

_____

_____

_____

_____

_____

_____

_____

_____

3. Do you believe that a particular kind of jealousy and competition is normal or healthy? Please reflect and write your thoughts about these actions.

_____

_____

_____

_____

_____

_____

_____

_____

4. Has anyone ever minimized your success? If so, write an essay explaining the incident and how you felt at the time. Please list your answers to the following questions: a) How did you navigate through it? b) What was the outcome?

_____

_____

_____

_____

_____

_____

_____

_____

CHAPTER 3

WOMEN, TAKE A STAND

"Go, gather together all the Jews who are in Susa, and fast for me. Do not eat or drink for three days, night or day. I and my attendants will fast as you do. When this is done, I will go to the king, even though it is against the law. And if I perish, I perish"
—Esther 4:16 (NIV).

One year after my licensure to the Gospel Ministry, I expressed to my pastor that I wanted to join the historical clergy organization in our city. The pastor told me that he would support me but it would be challenging because the organization had been an all-male group from its origin. Amazingly, I would become the FIRST female clergy to be accepted into the group.

As was the rule, my pastor wrote a letter of reference on my behalf, informing the clergy organization that he and the church had licensed me and that I was a member in good standing, very committed to the church and ministry. The pastor also explained that I had a "passion" for ministry and would be attending a religious program that would help prepare me further for ministry. He stated that I had strong leadership skills and would be a great asset to the organization.

With the reference letter in hand, I attended the clergy meeting. My pastor was supposed to have participated in the meeting, but he was in college himself and couldn't make it that night. Upon arrival, I announced myself and two well-seasoned group members escorted me to another room, where they interviewed me. I thought I would become a member that night, but the powers that be decided that they would wait and would let me know something at a later date. Remember, the male clergy didn't have to wait before becoming members. I heard part of the discussion and could discern that I would be placed on hold for a while.

Overcoming Doubts and Insecurities

After I left the conference room that night, I felt the anointing of strength and patience. Spiritually, emotionally, and mentally, I took a position— saying to myself I would return to the meeting place every month until the membership would vote and accept me as a member. There was a hallway with chairs for latecomers; I would sit until I was heard, approved, and accepted into the membership.

Because of how the previous meeting ended, I was a little doubtful that I would be accepted the following month, but as mentioned earlier, I was going to wait and pray. So, when the next month rolled around, I returned to the meeting place with some anxiety. I had faith in God that he would work this out and give me the desires of my heart because I needed to collaborate with other ministers and pastors so that they could mentor me.

I was welcomed by the same committee that met me the first time. I was a little nervous, but not that much, because I believed the Holy Spirit had given me a plan to follow. The committee asked me a few additional questions this time, and I answered them satisfactorily. Then, the president of the organization sent for the committee and me. I felt my heart slip into my throat. I was prepared for the worst. But when I entered the conference room, I saw a few gentle smiles and stern faces. I silently repeated one of my favorite scriptures, "For God has not given us a spirit of timidity, but a spirit of power, of love and of self-discipline" (2 Tim. 1:7 NIV).

The president congratulated me and welcomed me to the Body. I was given the right hand of fellowship, and it appeared that I was received by most. I was a happy soul! Also, I was the FIRST FEMALE MINISTER to join the illustrious organization. It meant a lot to me to be accepted into this group of clergies because I felt that I could progress in ministry by being in their presence, listening and adhering to their instructions and teachings, and taking note of their experiences and journeys.

I had my doubts and insecurities during the early years of ministry. Growing up in a male-dominated society made me doubt myself to some degree. I really couldn't see how I was going to be accepted into the ministry based on the way women ministers were viewed and treated back in the day. Typically, not many women held leadership roles in the church unless they founded a church or their husbands were pastors. In the early 80s, I only knew of two women pastors—one in North Carolina and the other in my area. Consequently, they had planted their own churches. Basically, women in that era were recognized more as evangelists, sisters, and mothers of the church. All of which I did not feel called to be. In short, this is why I felt doubtful that I would be accepted in a non-bias traditional ministry.

However, I was not going to allow tradition to dictate what I believe that God had put in me at my very conception of life. What actions did I take? I remained on the path that God placed me. Even with doubts and fears, I knew without a doubt that God had called me to authorized ministry. I accepted and acknowledged the call that God had on my life. I believed it, and I took a position and continued in the name of Jesus, praying, studying, preaching, and teaching the Word of God. I am grateful to God for inserting all the right people and resources that I needed to move forward in ministry.

At the outset of my call to ministry, I was not as academically prepared for professional ministry as those in the ministerial fellowship. So, the lack of experience coupled with no seminary training permeated me with insecurity. Listening to other ministers' conversations reminded me that I needed to complete my undergrad studies to move on to seminary. To become a well-rounded person in ministry, I knew I needed to broaden my knowledge by studying theology, psychology, sociology, and physiology.

As I continued the educational process, I began to feel more knowledgeable and comfortable conversing with educated and trained ministers. It took me a while, but I eventually enrolled in seminary and received my M.Div. and D.Min. Once I prepared myself, I no longer felt doubtful, insecure, or inferior to anyone.

The Strength of Women in Biblical Leadership

I have shared with you some of the leadership stances I have taken over the years of my ministry. Now, I will lift the leadership practices of at least three women in the Old Testament: Miriam, the sister of Moses, Deborah, and Esther.

Miriam: She was a leader in her own right. While there are several instances of Miriam serving in leadership roles in the Bible, I will focus only on one of her significant leadership experiences.

Miriam went down in biblical history as a poetess, singer, and prophetess. Like many people that God has called to do ministry, he chose Miriam as a leader, role model, and voice of inspiration and encouragement to the women of Israel (Herbert Lockyer, *"All The Women of The Bible,"* p 112).

As depicted in scripture, during the Red Sea experience, Miriam played the tambourine and sang, she courageously led the women and children dancing through the Red Sea—as the power of God parted the waters—making dry ground, so they all crossed over to safety (Exodus 15: 19-21).

Deborah: This prophetess and leader in the book of Judges was a pillow of strength and power. She was the wife of Lapidoth. Deborah was fearless, a force to be reckoned with and took her stance. According to the scripture, she led a general to war because he was too cowardly to go to war without her. She did not allow anything or anyone to shake her or break her down. Deborah was well known throughout the province for her strength and judgment and prophecy. She was a prominent leader of Israel and provided counseling and prophesy to the Israelites under the palm of Deborah.

Esther: We take note of our brave woman in the Bible named Esther. This courageous woman of God was chosen to be the wife of King Ahasuerus due to her grace and beauty. By the hand of God, Esther was selected from among all maidens in the land. Although she was a Jew, the King gave Esther much power and authority.

Haman, a servant of the king, had conspired to kill all Jews in the land. Mordecai, who had raised Esther, informed her of the plan. He pleaded with Esther to intercede to prevent the Jews from being destroyed.

Even though Esther could lose everything she had gained, she risked it all to partition the king to reverse his plan to save the Jews. Her reply was, "If I perish, I perish." She obeyed Mordecai and convinced the king.

At significant risk to Esther's comfort and wealth, God stepped in and changed the king's heart, saving her people.

Esther was the epitome of a great leader. She did what any good leader would have done, she took a stand for the right thing and saved a nation of people (Esther 2-5, NIV).

Chapter Summary:

- Women have significant contributions to make in leadership roles, both in historical and modern contexts.

- Confidence, persistence, and faith are key to overcoming barriers and doubts in leadership positions.

- Unity and support among women, particularly in ministry, are crucial for fostering growth and success.

- Celebrating each other's achievements and offering guidance helps create a supportive and empowering environment for all.

Self-Reflection:

1. As a leader, have you ever had to take a stand during a situation? Please describe the circumstance. Explain what you had to do to make it right.

_____

_____

_____

_____

_____

_____

_____

_____

2. If the leaders of a club, church, or an organization denied you membership, what would you do? Give details about how you would handle the rejection. Would you get an attitude?

_____

_____

_____

_____

_____

_____

_____

_____

3. Have you felt inferior to anybody that you have associated with? How did you discover that you were inferior? What specific details made you feel inferior to the person (s)?

_____

_____

_____

_____

_____

_____

_____

_____

_____

4. Identify at least three leaders in the Bible. You may select men or women. Please write at least three leadership traits that you share with that leader. If you do not share any likeness, list the traits.

_____

_____

_____

_____

_____

_____

_____

_____

_____

5. When you perceive doubt in yourself, can you recognize what brings about the doubt? If so, were you able to overcome your feeling of doubt?

_____

_____

_____

_____

_____

_____

_____

_____

_____

CHAPTER 4

NAVIGATING THESE RELIGIOUS WATERS

"In all your ways acknowledge Him,
And He shall direct your paths"
—Proverbs 3: 6 (NKJV).

In addition to my many rejections in ministry, I have listed four verbatim case studies that illustrate what four other female ministers have experienced along the lines of rejections and challenges that were incited by individuals in local churches and seminaries. Also, there are three case studies from men in leadership whom I know very well. I respect their experiences and voices.

The four case studies will give you a glimpse of what the four women ministers have experienced. I have included them so that you can read and reflect on some of the biases that will continue to exist in 2025.

As you read, whether you are in ministry or being inspired to ministry, insert yourself and experience the hurt and rejection that these godly women have experienced. Do not be discouraged, for God brought us through this degrading rhetoric and He will surely bring you through. *Selah.*

I have grown and developed from my personal struggles and rejections. Once you hear the negative side and see someone else's struggles that should help you to be better prepared for your ministerial journey. Thereby enabling you to be more counterproductive in all that you do for yourself and the Lord.

Case Study #1

Minister 1: "The biggest challenge I face in Church Tradition is simply being a female. I have come to accept that women in leadership will always be defending her call whether it's to a male or another female.

However, over my 15-plus years in ministry, I've learned to listen before responding with a defense. Just recently, there was an incident in which a member of our trustee ministry questioned my call into ministry. He wanted me to show him exactly where in scripture it says God has called a woman to preach.

In my early years of ministry, my response would have been, "It's everywhere in scripture." But as

I've matured and learned to listen to what the person was really asking; my responses have changed. This time I responded with another question. I said, "That depends, how big is your God?" I further explained. "I serve a Big God; he can't be limited because He is sovereign. He doesn't need human approval or permission. He does what He wants to, how He wants to, and when He wants to." The trustee simply chuckled and walked away. Granted this wasn't my first run in with this particular trustee, nor will it be my last.

We tend to focus on the gender-female, instead of the God behind it all. I believe that if we are willing to listen, keep an open dialogue and adapt to what God is doing, the church would be able to balance respect for tradition with a desire for progress and inclusivity."

Case Study #2

Minister 2: "When I first believed I was called to the ministry, I was rejected and told I didn't know what I was talking about. In fact, I was told that my calling would've been told to my pastor if I was truly called, and because he didn't have confirmation, I needed to wait. I thought he knew what he was talking about. I waited, but while waiting, I started to doubt my calling. I fell into unbelief when so many in my church were praying against me and making me feel like an outcast. I had members coming to tell me my place was in the choir, but I left the church for a little while because I needed to learn the truth about what I should do. The year I was gone, I learned more about discipleship, fasting, praying, and how the foundations were. I found the Holy Spirit within me during that time, but I had many people telling me if I didn't come back to church, I would be in a great world of trouble. I was rejected and abused by them. They said it was shameful that I left church and took my children. That we would be lost. I stayed away until God sent me back.

I went back not knowing if I'd be preaching or not. I constantly heard from the Lord to go back to school and I finished my bachelor's and master's degrees. I stayed loyal and humble despite my family turning on me. They made me feel like I shouldn't have a mind of my own. At times, I felt as if I was in a cult. I didn't feel like I was learning the truth about God's Word. It seems to be more about praising God through song. Don't get me wrong, it's good to praise Him through song, but I needed more. I craved learning about the spiritual disciplines, spiritual gifts, and how to be obedient to God's Word and living His truth. As I studied, I became more loyal, but I continued to watch and pray. I prayed for my church and the many visions that I had forgotten about. I began to remember all that God told me. One day, my pastor told me I haven't forgotten about you. I waited for ten years and I had gotten to the point of thinking maybe my place really was in the choir. I never stopped studying, learning, watching, and praying. God sent me to preach healing.

As I began my ministry, all I can say is I felt so alone. When I preached about the gifts of the Spirit, fasting, discipleship and moving outside of the church walls, I was criticized in the pulpit. I was tortured by my pastor because my messages were not ten minutes long. He stated that he says what needs to be said and sits back down. Because I was teaching something different and bringing the church to a new way of living, I was so called being "put in my place." At first, it hurt deeply because he was not only my grandfather, but he was my pastor. I didn't know how to feel about all the backlash coming from the pulpit from his mouth, but God told me to look at Him and know that I am loved. I stood firm on God's promises in the middle of my pain and torment, and I preached everything the

Lord gave me to preach. I had probably three individuals who were continuously praying and encouraging me because they saw what I was going through. I'm grateful that God placed the people I needed in my corner to help me to keep moving forward. This was a spiritual battle. It wasn't my family, but the enemy using them to try to steal, kill, and destroy my destiny. The power of the Lord has kept me still in the midst of my enemies. That familiar spirit was prayed down. People began to recognize that the call on my life is real, including my pastor. When teaching something they can't wrap their heads around, I do get scolded. I know that I know I'm preaching and teaching God's truth and it's convicting them. When the backlash comes, I see the need to pray harder for God to heal our land and help people to humble themselves. Turn from their wicked ways and know that God is God all by Himself. When we learn to truly trust and depend on God rather than our own strength, the better our lives will be: in the freedom of God. The move of God in our church is amazing. I'm so thankful that in the midst of feeling rejected, abused and having people turn their backs on me, I didn't give up. I trusted that God will do the work as I continued and I'm so thankful that in the midst of feeling rejected and abused by people's words and turning their backs on me, I didn't give up. I trusted that God would do the work as I continued to preach His Word."

Case Study #3

Minister 3: "My last year in seminary – second semester – ready to graduate – and the answer to a question in the Dean's class – throws some of us for a loop.

Challenge: The Dean asks a regular question: "How do we obtain 'salvation'?" Before anyone else could answer, a Muslim girl spoke and said that there were multiple ways to achieve salvation/to get to God/to claim eternal life/to save our souls:

I was outraged!! Did she not learn anything? Did she not understand? What was her theology?

To make 'bad' matters worse – she continued her comments by explaining the theory of the "MOUNTAIN" [we all are at the bottom— going up the "mountain" from different points we move up the "mountain" by doing different things to satisfy God (praying/working/serving/giving/ helping/loving)]. Of the 14 students in the class, three of us were appalled by her statements! The "SHOCKER" was that the Dean agreed with the Muslim girl. The three of us vehemently opposed her statements. It didn't matter where we were in our seminary journey or the rami-fications we could face from the Dean; we spoke out!!

We expressed our beliefs and what we had been taught and what the Holy Spirit had revealed to us...

We bombarded the Dean and the girl with Scriptures to support our beliefs: Luke 1: 68-69; Acts 4: 11-12; Revelation 7: 9-12.

They refused to relent – they tried to shake our faith, tried to make us doubt that our salvation comes only from Jesus the Christ.

Did they want us to preach to our congregations that the people could be "saved by works?"

There was no one to whom we could report these matters. After all, it was the Dean, himself, who supported the ideas!!"

Case Study #4

Minister 4: "As I ponder challenges that have impacted my ministry, one challenge immediately comes to mind. Because of that experience, I am always mindful of my approach to male ministers when visiting a church.

The challenge I am speaking of occurred when I was new in the ministry. As I entered ministry, there were no instructions or protocol given to follow when our church visited other churches.

We were just told our church would be visiting another church on said date.

One of the most hurtful incidents I have experienced occurred when our church had an afternoon service at another local church. Several male ministers were walking in the hallway of the church towards the pastor's office. They entered the pastor's office. When I, and another female minister approached the door, the host pastor shut the door in our faces. I am sure he saw us. The other ministers were so engaged in "good old boy talk" they did not appear to be aware of what was happening.

How did I cope with this? I prayed and asked God to help me represent him well as I dealt with feeling disrespected and rejected as a minister. I politely sat in the fellowship hall and rejoined the ministers as they exited the pastor's office to enter the sanctuary. Rejoining the ministers was my way of saying, "I am still here."

The experience helped me to realize that as a minister I am not to let the "good old boy syndrome" and those who do not want female ministers around define who I am as a minister. God has called me to ministry and that must be my focus regardless of the thoughts and beliefs of others, be it male or female."

Case Studies from Men in Ministry that I know and respect:

Case Study #5 Leaders must Lead:

Leadership is not gender specific. "So God created humanity in his own image, in the image of God created He him; male and female created He them." (Genesis 1:26-27 KJV).

There is no suggestion in scripture or the history of Christ's people that the gifts of the Spirit are distributed along gender lines. Many of our behaviors come from a patriarchal society where it was common in villages, communities and in the Church where males dominated the pulpit and preached to the people. Many individuals continue to hold up these outdated traditions to the degree that in some cases they perpetuate a myth that has been long debunked. Individuals hold on to the various traditions because it makes them comfortable, and the fear of progress may collide with the obvious.

We have heard of many women who have been ignored or discriminated against by the Church and society. Particularly within the Church. Many men still hold to their teaching that a woman should not teach or preach to a man.

Let's look at Deborah:

Deborah is a prophet and judge in the Bible. Deborah was a prophetess who spoke on God's behalf. Deborah was a charismatic military leader who led Israel to victory over their enemies. In the military it is a clear example of male-dominated leadership. Yet, Deborah was given charge over an Army.

Women bring spiritual depth, a nurturing spirit, and their ability to relate which sometimes are deficits in a male-dominated leadership environment. We've heard from many women who have been discriminated against in church leadership. "When a church doesn't welcome qualified women into leadership it's harmful to the identity and dignity of women and girls and it affects how they're treated by men and boys. Furthermore, it can cause damage to the Church environment" (Bill Gaultiere).

Deborah spoke on behalf of the Lord. She was called upon to deliver Israel from the hand of her enemies. If a woman can command an army: if she can speak on behalf of the Lord; then she can lead in any circumstance or condition. Israel was blessed with a great General named Barak. Barak understood that the Lord's leadership was with Deborah. Under God's guidance she sent for Barak who knew that

God's hand was with Deborah. Barak declared "if you go with me, I will go; but if you don't go with me, I won't go." (Judges 4:8)

Deborah was said to hear God's voice and share God's Word with others. As a priestess, she did not offer sacrifices, as the men did, but she did lead worship services and preach. There are several women in the New Testament who functioned as pastor-teachers. Priscilla, a close friend and coworker of Paul, was one of them.

I believe that the denial of women in leadership is a human concoction, not a divine one. Whether it be in the Boardroom, Government or in the Church, she is called to lead.

GOD > ∀

Rev. Dr. Edward Davis, MBA, CNPM

Conference Minister & Chief Executive Southern Conference UCC

Case Study #6

I am writing this case study at the request of the author and to honor my late mother who transitioned on August 6, 2024.

If ministry as Paul discusses in 2 Corinthians Chapters three and four as proclaiming or sharing the gospel of Jesus Christ by means of clay vessels, then who has the authority or makes the decision as to which vessel is to fulfil this awesome task?

Can a woman preach the gospel? According to the church environment in which I grew up the answer was no! It was my understanding that God did not call women to preach. As a result, there were no women preachers in the church. If memory serves me well, I do recall my pastor allowing women serving as pastors from other denominations to preach in the pulpit. I considered that to be a contradiction, however, I dared not question it.

It was not until 2007, under new pastoral leadership when the first woman was licensed to preach the Gospel of Jesus Christ in my home church. Following the sudden passing of the previous pastor, the next woman licensed to preach was my mother on October 31, 2022, under the current pastor. Although it was fifteen years between the first and second woman licensed to preach, we still can praise God that the church environment is changing for women who sense a calling on their life to preach the Gospel.

My first encounter with women in the preaching ministry was as a student at the now closed Bishop College located in Dallas, Texas. At that time, this church-related HBCU liberal arts institution had an estimated enrollment of 2,000 students which included approximately 300 young preachers from various denominations. They came from across the United States of America. Among the preachers, there were a small number of women preachers matriculating at the school. Personally, I do not recall having a problem with the women identifying themselves as preachers or questioning their call to ministry. The lack of a problem or questioning their call could possibly be due to my own soul-searching regarding preaching. Even to this day, I stay before the Eternal regarding my own call to ministry.

Upon attending and graduating from the Samuel DeWitt Proctor School of Theology at Virginia Union University in Richmond, Virginia, I encountered more women in ministry. They were associated with various denominations: Baptist, Holiness, and Methodist. All of them ministered on some level within their respective churches with several becoming pastors of churches. The Minister of Christian Education at the church where I attended was a woman and later was licensed to preach. Although I had been preaching longer, she became my big sister and often provided me with wise counsel. As a pastor, I licensed a woman to preach.

I return to the question raised at the beginning: Who decides which "clay vessel" is tasked to proclaim the good news of Jesus Christ? My conclusion is God! The role of pastors and the church is to affirm both men and women who sense a calling on their lives to preach the good news of Jesus Christ. We must remember, the first clay vessels to proclaim that Jesus was alive were women. The angel said, "But go, tell his disciples and Peter that he is going before you to Galilee" (Mark 16:7).

Women In Ministry from a Male Perspective
By Dr. Jerome O. Lee
African American/African Churches
Coordinator, Baptist General Association of Virginia

Case Study #7

A key tenant of the United Church of Christ, a social justice focused denomination, to which I belong is this: that it is a church that is "united and uniting." It means that we are one body under Jesus Christ and that the goal of the church is to unite all under Jesus. A consequence of this belief rooted in John 17:21 is that the United Church of Christ is a radically inclusive denomination. It believes and urges that all people have a place under the headship of Jesus Christ. That all no matter how diverse in race, sex, ethnicity and culture, have a home, a future and a place in Jesus.

Why this is important in view of the author's book ***Called to Lead: Overcoming the Challenges of Ministry in a Male-Dominated Space as a Woman of Faith.*** It's important because women in many Christian denominations have been excluded from the possibilities of pastoral leadership and other roles based solely on a repressive misinterpretation and application of the biblical text. The same misinterpretation of the biblical text that once was used to justify slavery and the oppression of the black race. It's a destructive backwards theology that places the highest value on a white, male, capitalistic and patri-archal hierarchy that believes that global leadership has been given to them by God to subjugate all others.

In my ministry as a church executive, I've witnessed and helped women that left male-dominated denominations and ministries that refused to give them the opportunity to exercise their God given gifts of leadership. When they came to us, they were seeking ministerial standing and opportunity in the United Church of Christ to serve. To that end, I did my part to promote and help women to get into pastoral and other leadership positions. Today, I am happy to say that many of our churches in our local area, have female leadership serving as pastors and leaders including the author. It's part of our mission as a church, to help all who are called to leadership within the church no matter male, female, black, white, gay or straight to find a place within to do what God has called them to do.

It's by helping congregations to see the scriptures in an enlightened way that uplifts all people. It's the way of Jesus. One of my favorite scriptures reads: "Where the Spirit of the Lord is, there is liberty." Wherever people are free to be who God created them to be, wherever there is happiness, wherever there is peace, love and joy. The Lord is there. Women in the Bible like Deborah, Jael, Mary the mother of Jesus, Elizabeth, the Hebrew Midwives and many others refused to be held back leading the people of God to freedom, love and peace. It's by following them and women in history like Antoinette Brown honored by the United Church of Christ as one of the first women ordained in 1851 and offered a position as a minister of a congregational church in 1852. It's by following great women leaders like Sojourner Truth,

Harriet Tubman and Shirley Chisholm. It's by following leaders like our author, Rev. Dr. Madelene Beard who started a ministry called Deborah's Women In Ministry, Inc., with the goal of helping all women to develop and nurture their leadership skills.

Finally, to women who may feel hindered by a denomination, an organization or any situation, I would urge you to look to the many biblical, historical and modern examples of great women leaders that have overcome obstacles and glass ceilings to thrive. Learn from them, imitate their methods and start ministries that will once and for all bring down a male-dominated system for a few to a system of freedom, justice and equality for all.

Rev. Dr. John T. Myers
Associate Conference Minister
Eastern Virginia Association
Southern Conference UCC

Finding Balance Between Tradition and Progressive Leadership

I was raised in the traditional Baptist church; therefore, I have pretty much maintained the practices until the Coronavirus appeared in 2020.

Worship every Sunday, in person, was important to me. Also, physically attending all other services, Bible study, prayer meetings, and business meetings were expected in the traditional church.

To me, one of the most sacred moments in worship was celebrating the Lord's Supper. The communion was prepared by the Diaconate ministry, and they placed the element trays on the communion table. When the hour came, I would administer the elements with the assistance of the associate minister and Diaconate ministry. Morcover, I have struggled with the balance between setting up and serving communion the traditional way versus the progressive leadership methods that I would later come to perform due to the safety of the parishioners while COVID lingered in the atmosphere.

In my opinion, the Coronavirus has changed the fabric of the traditional church and ignited a more progressive leadership approach to doing church.

I recall so vividly when Rev. Dr. Edward S. Davis, our conference minister, informed the leaders of the churches that we had to consider other methods of worship, because COVID was life threatening and was not safe for us to meet in person. Indeed, that was a scary time for me. I was barely familiar with Zoom and knew less about social media.

While I felt the shift coming, I still didn't think too much about it until we, the pastors, had to choose another approach to worship and maintain our congregations.

They were hard and fast praying times for me as a pastor and leader. I realized that I had to do something to maintain my congregation because our church had done well, and I wanted to keep them moving forward.

Again, I was stressed over the pandemic and everything that I heard pressed heavily on me. I knew that God would provide, but I had to have more than faith. I put faith into action. I appointed a team from my congregation who had stronger technological skills than me. I had to learn more about Zoom before we started holding our training sessions. As the pastor, it was necessary for me to learn at least the basics about Zoom. With the help of God and the inspiration of the Holy Spirit, I went online and studied Zoom tutorials. I studied the tutorials night and day for three weeks straight. After which, the team and I started making plans to teach members of the congregation how to use Zoom, Facebook, and Givelify, all of which were important to the life of our local congregation. The team did very well with teaching and guiding others on how to use the various platforms. Tamaika Hamlin, our church administrator, did an outstanding job guiding and teaching the congregants how to use Givelify. Amazingly, our congregants never lost their momentum of giving. God is good! The church remained strong in the ministry of giving.

I am still basically a traditional pastor, but I have established some balance along with becoming a more progressive leader in my local church. I have experienced firsthand that change is inevitable. Notably, change can come at a moment's notice, and I must be prepared.

COVID was detrimental to the health and wellbeing of our congregations. It has helped me to embrace the following new approaches to doing ministry for such a time as this. What? The Lord's Supper is served in plastic bags and not from golden vessels! Prior to this time frame, I couldn't imagine such a thing.

BUT 1) I am slowly adapting to seeing the parishioners pick up the communion elements which were prepackaged in plastic bags before they arrived at church.

2) I have adjusted to holding worship services and meetings on Zoom and other platforms.

3) I love people and prefer to see them in person; however, I am adjusting to unique ways to suffice for not being in person.

And 4) giving via Givelify has become an easy and acceptable platform for giving to the church.

At present, my church does meet in person. However, we use different social media platforms for hybrid worship and meetings. And I continue to administer the Lord's Supper coupled with the parishioners receiving their prepackaged bags as they enter the sanctuary.

Trusting God's Guidance in Challenging Moments

In the mid-80s, I was a bi-vocational minister and had taken my vacation to attend the Hampton University Ministers' Conference. I arrived on a Sunday evening and checked into my dorm room. I rested for a while, got up and refreshed myself. Then, I headed to Ogden Hall where the Choir Guild held their opening musical. So, I was walking along the sidewalks, which led to Ogden Hall. I was inhaling and exhaling the fresh air that smelled of the huge magnolia blossoms on the trees. I was happy and felt on top of the world. Not a worry or a fear at hand. My mind was lofty. I vividly recalled my first year attending the Hampton University Ministers' Conference and Choir Guild. That was an exciting time for me because I had been told so much about the conference and what to expect. But little did I know, my spirits would be crushed by someone who obviously did not believe that women should be ministers.

I meandered my way through Ogden Hall, looking for a seat where I could enjoy the music and the renowned guest singers. I walked past a gentleman who was already seated in the same row. Once I settled in, he looked down the row at me—pointing at my name badge—saying, "What's that?" I said, "What do you mean, "What's that?" Then, he pointed directly at my name and said, "Who is that?" I said, "Why, that is my name." He proceeded to smirk at me. So, I looked at his badge and said, "And who is that?" He said, "That's my name and I am a minister." I in turn, pointed at my badge, and said, "This is my name, and I am a minister, too." He appeared to have become agitated; bounced up and walked briskly away while murmuring something under his breath. He looked back with frustration on his face. I stared at him until he was out of sight. I felt like I had been hit by a boomerang— all the excitement suddenly drained from me. Tears even welled in my eyes. I got up and moved to a more isolated area, so no one would see me crying. I sat and listened to the program and the testimonials of some of the singers. In the meantime, I opened my Bible to Psalm 121 and read in its entirety. I cited "I look to the hills from whence cometh my help, and all of my help cometh from the Lord."

Rejection can be a hard pill to swallow. One must be anchored in the Lord and grounded in the Word of God to prevent you from withdrawing from the plans that God has made for you. I have experienced many rejections during my 38 years of ministry, and I know that it was nobody but God that kept me moving forward in ministry. No matter what, I continued to press forward because I knew God would be my guide and cover me in all that I would do for him.

Let me share some of my experiences of rejection with you. Some may be surreal, but true. Read on, if you will.

Rejection by a Baptist Organizational Leader

I had been teaching a class for a Baptist organization a few years before I preached my initial sermon. Once the organizational leader was told that I had preached my initial sermon, he told my local church liaison that he no longer needed me. In other words, I could teach as "Mrs." Beard, but not as "Rev." Beard. I was disappointed, but it did not destroy or prevent me from going forward in ministry.

I became a convenient statistic for churches during the search and call process. Unknowingly, I was called to preach at churches going through their search and call process. This was a process that the church used to interview and qualify pastors for pastoral positions.

At least three churches have called me to supply the pulpit in the past. Once I finished the preaching assignment, I received a letter of denial five to ten days later. No, I never applied to any of the churches in the first place. Thus, this was humiliating because I was unaware that I was being considered for a pastoral candidate. After getting the second letter, I realized I was a "convenient statistic" for rejection. "It appeared that the church probably needed to document persons they interviewed and denied for some accountability purposes," I thought.

Someone stated that, "In this life some rain must fall." I believe it is safe to say that the average person would like to hear all the positive and encouraging things that can be said about any given situation.

However, we should give an ear to the negative side of life, if only for a short time, so you can see what is being expressed and experienced by others.

Remember that change is inevitable. Change can be good or indifferent. It is up to you how you embrace and accept change. Pray and draw from the Lord because He is the greatest change agent of biblical history.

Chapter Summary:

- Change is inevitable and can be good or indifferent, depending on how it is embraced.
- Drawing strength from the Lord, who is the greatest change agent in biblical history, is essential.
- Personal struggles and rejections provide growth and development.
- Hearing others' struggles can prepare and equip one better for their ministerial journey.
- Encourages current and aspiring ministers not to be discouraged by rejection but to trust that God will guide them through challenges.
- Emphasizes the importance of being anchored in the Lord and grounded in His word to navigate through rejection and challenges.

Self-Reflection:

1. After reading this chapter, do you believe that something positive can come out of rejection? Yes, or no? Explain your answer in detail.

_____

_____

_____

_____

_____

_____

_____

_____

_____

_____

2. Do you find solace in knowing that other clergy persons have been rejected in ministry? Does this help you or not? If so, please explain.

_____

_____

_____

_____

_____

_____

_____

_____

_____

3. Name the most challenging moment that you have experienced in the ministry. How did you navigate through that period? Please describe it in detail.

_____

_____

_____

_____

_____

_____

_____

_____

_____

4. Knowing that change is inevitable, how do you react to change? Give an incident of change that you embraced. How did you feel about making the change? Did you embrace or reject the change? Describe how you embraced change. If you did not embrace change, explain why you did not.

_____

_____

_____

_____

_____

_____

_____

_____

_____

CHAPTER 5

I ANSWERED THE CALL, NOW WHAT?

Then I heard the voice of the Lord saying, "Whom shall I send? And who will go for us?" And I said, "Here am I. Send me!"—Isaiah 6:8 (NIV).

Once I completed my education at the community college level, I thought I was well on my way to being satisfied and that everything I wanted to accomplish was falling in place inch by inch. Then, I had this quest to continue my education. I was seeking a professional career in teaching, with the intent of becoming a college professor. But I realized that something was going on within me. "I was happy enough," I thought. But there was something stirring deep down inside my soul that kept me longing and reaching for something that I was not receiving or giving. It was a restlessness, if you will. I found myself constantly thinking about church and the ministry. I started gravitating to other ministers, associating with them. I began attending other churches' special programs. I would listen to other ministers preach and observe them in almost every way one could think of. Although I did a lot of visiting, I remained loyal and devoted to my home church because I did not want to break the sacred trust that I had with my pastor and church family.

I became more restless. I started having dreams whereby I was following Jesus, but I could never see His face; only the back of Him, His sandals, and His footprints in the sand. This went on for months and months. The same recurring dream or vision.

By now, my inspirations had advanced to a higher plane. I would wake up at night singing—sitting straight up in bed--singing, "He Looked Beyond My Faults and Saw My Needs." (Keep in mind I am not a singer) This, too, was a recurring and lofty experience. The melody and lyrics became etched in my spirit. By this time, I discerned that God was truly calling me to serve Him.

When I realized God was calling me to ministry, I was concerned about telling my husband. My husband was and is a man of faith, but he would share from time to time about a young lady that he used to like until she became an evangelist. After she became like until she became an evangelist. After she became an evangelist, he stopped talking to her. So, as I felt the spirit-stirring in my soul, I would get nervous about telling my husband that I felt called to ministry. Female clergy were not welcomed in ministry or leadership positions during the early 80s. It is sad to say that they are also not welcomed by some religious traditions and people today.

Letting go of "self" and the things that I enjoyed doing were critical at this juncture in my life. In retrospect, life was good, and my husband and I were doing well. It seemed like change was inevitable and fostering some issues. I started facing and adjusting to one change after another. I slowly came to grips with myself and the lifestyle my husband and I were living. I gave up the fabulous parties that we used to hold in our home on special occasions. These were classy events. I loved to entertain, and dance but I had to let go of the dancing. My Christian upbringing taught me, if you were 'saved' you didn't dance or go to parties. My husband was trying to adapt to all the changes I was making. My desire to transform into a godlier life had an impact on him. He wasn't always pleased with my changes because some of them affected his lifestyle.

I loved to dress and was very fashionable. High heels were my favorite. I wore makeup, expensive colognes. I went through a period where I felt that I needed to dress down. I loved to dress and wear high heels (now called stilettos). Some people were constantly telling me that I was too pretty to be a minister and that I should continue to enjoy life while I was young. Instead, I sacrificed my love for fashion and started wearing what I deemed to be appropriate attire for a Christian woman. Based on what others were saying, I needed to look more holy for God. So, I toned it down for Him. "Or was I trying to please the public?" I would say under my breath.

By this time, I was focused more on trying to respond to God's call on my life. I had the desire and hunger to do more and more for kingdom building. I prayed. I made daily notes of my actions, my thought processes, people's comments, and how I was going to plan to keep my life moving from day to day. It was evident that I wanted to please God and follow Him and the leadership of the Holy Spirit.

Practical Steps for Beginning the Journey

In the same way you plan for secular careers, I was planning my journey under the leadership of the Holy

Spirit and the voice of God through the Scriptures. I have found that the following steps would be most helpful as you journey in ministry:

- Prayer is always the beginning of your journey with the Lord.

- Meditate on God's Word.

- Be able to recognize God's calling on your life. Be sure you are not following your understanding but seek wisdom and knowledge from God.

- Do not allow other people to brainwash you into believing that God has called you when, in essence, He has not. God oversees your calling.

- Once you have established that God has called you, share your story with your pastor or spiritual leader.

- Do not be discouraged if you have not discerned your form of ministry yet.

- Seek direction and insight from your pastor.

- Know your denomination's policy and protocol concerning authorizing women in ministry, especially leadership roles in the church.

- If you do not have a mentor, look for a support group, mentor, or spiritual leadership coach.

- Approach ministry from a male's perspective because it gives you a stronger level of confidence and respect, especially among your male contemporaries.

- Do not wear your feelings on your shoulders—you can't be timid.

- Be prepared to stand alone.

- Be the lady that God created you to be—maintain your femininity.

- Prepare yourself academically, both for ministry and secular careers.

- After you have exhausted all traditional measures for leadership in ministry, consider moving to another denomination that supports women ministers in leadership.

- Be a life-long learner.

Seeking God's Direction For Your Ministry

As you seek God's direction for your ministry, I encourage you to read and adhere to the following advice:

Maintain Your Integrity. It is critical for clergy women to maintain their integrity as they feel called to ministry, especially, if you are reaching for higher heights. I have learned during my listening experiences; you must be cognizant that you may be manipulated by some men in higher places, and possibly some women, also. You are likely to be taken advantage of if you look or act desperate. Predators can spot you a mile away if you are desperate and want something bad enough. Men in higher positions knowing you are trying to get there as well might take advantage of you. Always be aware, observant and cautious. Draw from your God-given wisdom. Do not allow bling, hype, position, and status to slay your spirit and reputation.

If you feel you are not progressing in ministry as fast as you like, be patient, prayerful, and trust God. He will elevate you in due time; your season will come. You may have to take a non-traditional route sometimes, but that's ok. Do not get caught in a trap of broken promises. Do not allow yourself to be used and abused. Maintain your dignity.

Avoid Gossip. Stay out of the gossip circles. They will get you nowhere but in a circle of confusion. Remember, what you share in confidence will often end up in the ear of someone else's friend. They also have friends who will keep the gossip moving. When you hear it again, not only are you accursed of repeating it, but it would have manifested into something huge and detrimental. That's when friendships and professional relationships become destroyed.

Do Not Succumb to Compliments. It's encouraging to receive compliments after you have dressed your best, made your best speech, sang your favorite song, or preached your best sermon. However, I suggest you not get excited about flowery words and superficial compliments. Sadly, some people do not mean what they say. You do not want an inflated ego, for it is empty and meaningless and supports no foundation for the manifestation of the Holy Spirit.

In this life, even your friends can be cruel in that they will praise you after you give a speech or preach God's Word. They will have you thinking you are perfect and do not need anything but to open your mouth and sing or preach, and the Lord will do the rest. In reality, having more training, education, and experience would be best.

Protect Your Time. I will address time management in more depth later in this book. Consequently, I must mention it at this interval. Managing time has been a challenge for me most of my ministry. I cannot stress how important it is for you to keep a planner/calendar to balance all your activities. Keeping the planner is not enough. Do check the planner daily and follow through with the appointments or assignments. Maybe you haven't gotten that busy yet, but the time will come when you must protect your time, which means you schedule your events or time with your family and stick to it. You must protect your time because other people will disrupt your schedule and time, and you will not know what happened. Be intentional about protecting your time.

In short, this chapter describes part of my call story and how I had to adapt to change; I had one plan for my life, but God had another.

Do Not Be Illusive; The Struggle in Ministry is Real. Some people experience a few struggles, while others experience more difficult life-changing ones. Note that everything that looks like a well-oiled machine is not. Some of us cope with more disap-pointments and adjustments than we can imagine.

I also listed practical steps for those aspiring to or already in ministry. I hope you will be more comfortable with your overall life once you take these steps.

Lastly, adhere to maintaining your integrity, avoid gossip, and do not put your trust in compliments. And always remember to protect your time. *Selah.*

Chapter Summary:

- Embrace the unexpected changes in life as part of God's plan.

- Understand that struggles in ministry are real and varied.

- Follow practical steps to navigate ministry effectively.

- Uphold integrity, avoid gossip, and manage time wisely.

- Always prioritize your spiritual journey and stay grounded in faith.

Self-Reflection:

1. After reading this chapter, can you explain your call story? If so, describe it step by step.

_____

_____

_____

_____

_____

_____

_____

_____

_____

_____

2. Has God changed your direction at any time in your life? What did you do? Explain.

_____

_____

_____

_____

_____

_____

_____

_____

_____

3. The author has suggested practical steps to follow as you journey into ministry. Name and expand on five of them. Which one could you benefit most?

_____

_____

_____

_____

_____

_____

_____

_____

_____

4. How would you avoid engaging in the conversation if you were among others gossiping? Explain.

_____

_____

_____

_____

_____

_____

_____

_____

_____

CHAPTER 6

CHECK YOUR MOTIVES

"If anyone will not welcome you or listen to your words, leave that home or town and shake the dust off your feet—"
"I am sending you out like sheep among wolves. Therefore, be as shrewd as snakes and as innocent as doves" –Matthew 10: 14, 16 (NIV).

I probably wouldn't have gone into ministry if it had been left up to me. My goal was to become a teacher and ultimately become a college professor. But God led me down another path. I obeyed Him, which is the first attribute he looks for in leaders.

I did not call or send myself into ministry, if this makes sense. I did not have ulterior motives or anything like that as a part of my plan for entering the Lord's ministry. I didn't have magic under my sleeves to go into ministry to work healing or magic. There is no unethical or vicious plan in my heart or soul to deceive or defile God's plan for me.

While I was not anxious about answering the call to the ministry, my ministry happened by a natural progression.

Let's revisit my childhood. My family and the church leaders always volunteered me to recite poems and read scripture. I was around eight years of age. So, I had no choice; I would do as they said if they wanted me to read scripture, and I did that.

A season came when the saints started teaching me how to pray. That seemed to have been so natural for me. Thank God! There I was-- reading scripture and praying not only at my church (my childhood church in North Carolina) but I did the same thing at other churches. People thought seeing a young child read and pray was amazing. Accordingly, reading God's Word and praying became an intricate part of my life.

I was always preaching and reading scriptures to my siblings at night. At least three or four times a week, I would set up my altar, a cardboard box almost as tall as me. My siblings would get tired of me sometimes, but for the most part, they gathered around me and listened to my spiritual offerings. As I reflect on those days, I realize that they were some special times for me. God was using me then, but I did not know His plan.

With the Lord's progressive will, I became a secretary for the Sunday school during my early teens. I was a member of the Youth Choir and Youth Ushers Ministry. Later, I joined the Missionary Circle and the Senior Choir. Finally, the Lord called me to the ministry. I served as an associate minister at my home church in Suffolk, Virginia, and ministered at other churches until Galatians United Church of Christ called me to be their servant leader.

My ministerial journey has bloomed beautifully and has not been composed of motives. Indeed, God ordered my steps from childhood through adulthood.

Leading in Alignment with God's Will

I believe that God wants us to lead with faith and integrity. The story of Moses reminds me of when God called him to lead the children of Israel out of Egypt. First, Moses had a spirit of insecurity and did not feel significant enough to do what God asked. Second, Moses procrastinated because he thought his speech was not eloquent enough to lead. But God assured him that everything would be alright. All Moses had to do was lean and depend on God's strength and wisdom. Even with Moses' doubts and infirmities, he obeyed God's will (Exodus 3-4 KJV). Thus, obedience is a fundamental attribute in leadership. With that said, I have always led with an obedient spirit. God truly blesses us in ways you never dream of when you are obedient.

Biblical Support for Godly Leadership

Jesus was a servant leader and taught His disciples to lead by following Him. Jesus was the ultimate role model in leadership. To summarize Matthew 20: 25-28 (KJV), Jesus taught His disciples that they were not to rule or have authority over the people. If there were great people among them, they were to become servants. Genuine servant leaders will lead with pure hearts, humility, and grace.

Over the years, I have led my congregation by obeying God. I do not always get it right, but God is the head of my life. I have been inspired to lead with love and humility, constantly exercising grace and mercy where others are concerned.

Avoiding Selfish Ambitions (idol worship, notoriety, titles, and chasing money)

Listed below are four selfish ambitions that I strongly suggest that female ministers would avoid:

Idol Worship: One might think that idol worship does not exist today, but it does. You don't necessarily have to worship golden calves or gods as they did in the Old Testament days. In the 21st century, we idolize different objects and people. Here are several things that we may worship today: cell phones/ texting during worship. Many idolize iPads, Tik-Tok, Facebook, cars, houses, friends, or loved ones, just to name a few. You may ask, "How are these things idol worship?" My position is that anything you put before God or love more than God is "idol worship." As ministers, we must get our priorities in order. God comes first, and all other things come last. The Bible states, "Thou shalt have no other gods before me." (Exodus 20:3 KJV)

Notoriety: There are famous church leaders all over the world. I can't say if they worked or schemed to become accomplished notable leaders. In some cases, people become famous because they have earned it based on their service to the community and other contributions that they have made. On another note, notoriety is earned over time. It's called "paying your dues" in society.

Titles: There's nothing wrong with ministers having titles if they are earned, used from the proper perspective, and accurate. Some individuals are fussy about their titles, they will insult you if you do not address them by their preferred titles. I do not feel that strongly about titles. However, what disturbs me most is when people address the male contemporaries by their titles and don't give me the same courtesy. It's almost like they are intentionally trying to minimize me by referring to me as "Sistah," "Mrs," or my first name. Some women address their minister husbands with titles, but then, they will call me by my first name or refer to me as a "friend" as if they have known me for a lifetime. I have never understood that mindset, either. I have my way of dealing with those isolated situations, though. I smile and address them the same way they address me. They get the message, too.

From a biblical perspective, Jesus didn't use titles. His name was "Jesus," along with many other names. I don't recall in scripture where He complained about anyone addressing him as Jesus, Lord, Rabbi, Father, etc. Ask how they prefer to be addressed to avoid disrespecting a sister or fellow clergy.

Chasing Money: I assume that chasing money means the person loves money and is trying to make or win money through every initiative and possibly by any means necessary. You can also have an unhealthy love for money, which boils down to greed. "Being greedy causes trouble for your family, but you protect yourself by refusing bribes" (Proverbs 15: 27 CEV). Ministers should be careful when voicing their interests and concerns about making money and demanding a certain amount. I understand, however, that some ministers are career pastors, and that's how they care for their families. To me, that's a different story than "chasing money." I served my church for almost 14 years with very little income from them, and that was fine for us. We had an understanding, and I was a bi-vocational pastor as well. Then, I became a career pastor for the last 23 years. God has truly blessed us as pastor and congregation.

Sometimes at your sincerest, happiest, and joyous time, someone will question your motive or integrity for what God has done. About a month after I preached my initial sermon, an elderly lady who belonged to one of the churches in my local community approached me after a service one Sunday afternoon with a hurtful question. She said, "What are you trying to prove by entering the ministry? You need to find yourself something else to do." I was hurt because she was one of the ladies I looked up to and admired with all my heart. I smiled at her and said, "I am not trying to prove anything to anybody because God has called me into the ministry." I cried all the way home that day. However, that conflicting question did not keep me down. Once I returned home, I found my way to Philippians 4:8 (KJV) — "Finally, brethren, whatsoever things are true, whatsoever things are honest, whatsoever things are just, whatsoever things are pure, whatsoever things are lovely, whatsoever things are of good report; if there be any virtue, and if there be any praise, think on these things." This pericope of scripture has always encouraged me. The next thing I knew, my spirits were right back up. Praise God for His word!

Chapter Summary:

- Ensure your motivations for ministry are aligned with God's will and not personal gain.

- Emulate biblical leaders like Moses and Jesus, leading with humility, obedience, and integrity.

- Steer clear of idol worship, notoriety, titles, and the pursuit of money for selfish reasons.

- Maintain integrity, avoid gossip, manage your time, and be patient, trusting God to guide your ministry journey.

Self-Reflection:

1. Have you ever mentally questioned a minister or a trusted church member about what you believed to have the wrong motive (s) for being in ministry? Yes or No. Please explain what you witnessed or felt that brought that thought to mind. Did their actions or beliefs harm your spirit?

_____

_____

_____

_____

_____

_____

_____

_____

2. What does the expression "natural progression" in ministry mean from the readings? Use examples in your responses.

_____

_____

_____

_____

_____

_____

_____

3. List three leadership qualities that Jesus suggested in this chapter.

_____

_____

_____

_____

_____

_____

_____

_____

_____

4. Considering your religious culture, which one of the selfish ambitions do you hear about "most" often? Explain why. Which one do you hear least about? Explain why.

_____

_____

_____

_____

_____

_____

_____

_____

_____

CHAPTER 7

WALKING IN HUMILITY

"Do nothing out of selfish ambition or vain conceit, but in humility consider others better than your-selves"—Philippians 2:3 (NIV).

The role of humility in effective leadership has many facets. Let's take a moment to see what Nelson's New Illustrated Bible Dictionary says about humility. "Humility – a freedom from arrogance that grows out of the recognition that all we have and are comes from God. Humble people focus more on God and others than on themselves." (p. 586)

When I accepted the call to ministry, the term "humility" became an all-time favorite word of my pastor. He constantly reminded me about the importance of remaining humble. The pastor would say, "You must lay down 'self' and reflect more on the needs of people. Jesus's thoughts were on people and He lived His whole life for the good and salvation of others."

During my catechism, some of the Ecclesiastical Council members also discussed humility's meaning and importance as I moved up the ladder of life. They stressed that if I weren't humble, the church and the world would bring me to my knees and that I would always call on God.

The church elders were correct. The ministry and the church would undoubtedly make you humble. When the naysayers start talking, and the fiery darts land in your direction, you will call out Jesus' name. Amen.

I have tried to walk humbly in every facet of my life. Although I came from a dysfunctional family, I loved them more than life itself. I walked humbly with them through all our ups and downs. As I matured and developed into adulthood, I maintained respect for all humankind.

After the Lord blessed me to achieve the education I desired in life, I believe that I walk in humility stronger than ever. I know what God has done for me, so I owe Him all the glory, honor, and praise.

Learning from Biblical Examples of Humble Leadership

Here are three notorious leaders of the Bible that illustrate examples of humility:

First, as a boy, Moses became a prince and lived a privileged life in Pharaoh's palace. It is unbelievable that a man raised in splendor and wealth would have been humbled and submissive to God's will. That tells me that Moses had a good heart and was more concerned about saving and restoring a good quality of life to a remnant of God's people—the Israelites who had been oppressed. Moses was a wise and extraordinary leader. He was a man of God filled with humility at the outset of his spiritual journey.

I believe God called Moses to lead because he knew Moses would listen to him from the beginning of his call story. As stated in the previous chapter of this book, not only did God get Moses' attention through the burning bush, but he was obedient to God. There were times that Moses was startled, confused, and hesitant when he didn't feel comfortable with God's instructions. But he would overcome his shock, press for clarity, and keep progressing.

Moses displayed humility even when he approached God about his inadequacies and when God requested something of him. Humility appears when God asks Moses to go on various assignments for Him. Once God made his instructions clear to Moses, he would regain his confidence and was off to carry out God's assignments.

During Moses' most challenging times, he sought God for wisdom and understanding for his assignments. Moses was known for his humility and perseverance and always pressed forward with whatever God wanted him to accomplish.

Like Moses, some of us possess humility, but it may not be as powerful as his. It is also a possibility that we could be shocked at some occurrence that God is challenging us to do. Note that some of us have various levels of humility. Knowing ourselves well will help us recognize that we need to pray to God for more growth and strength. Our call to action is not to be weary because God will care for us and our situations.

Samuel is our second leader who demonstrated humility toward God and Israel. He was blessed and humbled before conception because his mother prayed earnestly for a child in her old age, and God gave him to her.

Samuel was a great man of God. He vowed to be holy and righteous unto the Lord. He served God as a prophet, intercessor, priest, and judge. In addition to being holy unto God, he was a faithful, prayerful man who loved and cared for humanity his whole life. (Lockyer, Herbert, pp.292-294. "All the Men in the Bible")

Third, Jesus was the personification of humility. While Jesus was conceived through the Holy Spirit, his earthly parents were humbled.

Scripture states that Jesus was placed in a feeding trough in a stable. That environment sets the stage for Jesus being born in humble beginnings and thus He continued to live that way until He died.

Jesus' humility took him to the cross, where he gave up His life to save a sin-sick world of sinners. He rose on the third day that those who believed in Him would have the right to eternal life. Thus, all who believe in His name shall be saved. I do not know another person who would have given his life for all humankind.

When I think about the magnitude of work our Lord did for us, I am encouraged to continue in His modality to nurture, love, and be a blessing to others as long as possible.

One of Paul's epistles bears a powerful reminder that we "Do nothing out of selfish ambition or vain conceit, but in humility consider others better than yourselves. Verse 4 seals it, each of you should look not only to your own interests, but also to the interests of others." (Philippians 2:3-4 NIV) *Selah*.

Cultivating a Servant's Heart

I was born the second oldest child in my family. I had an older brother who is now deceased. Because I was a girl, my younger siblings looked up to me for everything. I was the go-to person for all their needs and desires. Thus, leadership began in me at an early age.

My mother had a career in nursing, and she worked shifts. So, I became responsible and accountable for not only my siblings but the household as well. Even when my mother was off, if the children needed anything, she would tell them, "Go tell your sister." There I was, the leader of the pack. I would see that they were fed and clean. I washed dishes by hand and cleaned the house. When I got older, I prepared their meals as best as possible. For those who were in school, I assisted them with their homework.

When I was around thirteen, my mother told me it was time for me to learn how to pay bills. We lived in a rural area. The post office was about a mile from our home. Mama would make a list, give me the money, and send me to the post office once a month to purchase money orders. I didn't like what she told me to do at the time, but it taught me responsibility and the importance of paying bills. I used to think I was spoiling mama instead of her spoiling me. In essence, I became an adult early in my young life. By this time, I really felt like I was the leader of the household and the family. Everything going through me, especially where my siblings were concerned.

As a child, this time was very difficult for me but I naturally assumed a leadership role in my family. I was prayerful and read scriptures for encouragement and direction. Amazingly, I would catch a ride to church or walk approximately a mile or so to church all by myself. Going to church gave me inspiration and hope that I could continue to assist my mother with the children.

Once I became active in church, the elders recognized my leadership skills. As a youngster, I was asked to serve as secretary for the Sunday school. I volunteered to serve on the Usher's ministry. These assignments served as my leadership preparation and stepping stones to more advanced ministry in the local church.

I had cared for my siblings and mother for so long until I had cultivated a servant's heart. I loved my mother and siblings dearly and didn't want to see anything lacking. Life was not about me. Instead, my concerns and worries were always about how my siblings were fairing. As young as I was, I worried about my mother's safety while working at night. I was elated and relieved when I would hear my mother's car turn in the driveway either early in the morning or late at night, depending on which shift she worked. That took a lot of worry off my mind. My stepfather lived in the home, but I mainly communicated with my mother. I didn't have the best relationship with him. Being a tween, I always thought he took our mother away from us. I suppose that I was jealous or selfish at times. He was the father of the two youngest children, and there were two of us from my mother's and father's previous marriage. We were a blended family. We all got along, but I only took my orders from my mother.

In summary, having experienced a lifetime of nurturing my siblings, mother, and others has blessed me with a servant's heart. I will always desire to love and encourage not only my family but God's people.

Personal Experiences

When you know that you have worked hard, whether academically or through hands-on training/experience, you feel blessed to be addressed by the appropriate title. However, it is not the end of the world if you aren't given the title. I guess it is the "feminist "theology" in me when I am addressed as "Mrs" or "Ms." Many times, the addresser does not know if I am married or single. Their assumptions may be inadequate. All I am asking for is equality. Show me the same respect that you give to my male contemporaries.

As indicated earlier, I was taught by my pastor and other church leaders to be humble. I was mindful of walking in humility, and I still do. Over time, I have been a role model to female ministers by guiding them, recommending resources, making special donations, and sacrificing my time to help them.

On one occasion, I had a friend who stated that I was her mother in ministry and that she highly respected me. She told me often that I was the best teacher for her. She started a new church and needed a lot of support. I tried to help her by recommending that she do certain things or not do certain things (i.e., don't move so fast, do not be demanding of your congregants, and do not expect people to leave their churches to join or support your ministry, etc.). As I reminded her of certain things we had discussed, she would say, "I got this." Where is the humility here? It's missing because her reply was filled with arrogance. So, in essence, when someone says, "I got this," they are depending on their knowledge and strength."

Chapter Summary:

- Embrace humility as essential to effective leadership, understanding it as freedom from arrogance and recognizing that all comes from God (Nelson's New Illustrated Bible Dictionary, p. 586).

- Learn from the humility of Moses, who, despite his upbringing, humbly obeyed God's call to lead the Israelites out of Egypt (Exodus 3-4). Follow Samuel's example, dedicated to God from birth, serving with humility and devotion (1 Samuel 1-7). Emulate Jesus, the ultimate model of humility, born in a stable and sacrificing himself for humanity's salvation.

- Cultivate a servant's heart through early responsibilities and leadership roles, fostering a deep care for family and community needs. Draw strength from church involvement, preparing for broader ministry through service and dedication.

- Advocate for equality in ministerial titles, emphasizing respect and fairness in addressing peers. Guide others with humility, offering mentorship and support while encouraging reliance on God's wisdom and guidance. Address challenges in leadership with grace, promoting humility over self-reliance and fostering a spirit of learning and growth.

Self-Reflection:

1. Now that you understand humility from a biblical perspective, how would you describe it before reading this chapter? Explain and give two examples of what you believe humility to be before.

_____

_____

_____

_____

_____

_____

_____

_____

_____

_____

_____

_____

_____

2. Can you name someone in real life who depicts humility from a godly view? If so, do you mind sharing who they are and what their traits are?

_____

_____

_____

_____

_____

_____

_____

_____

_____

3. Ministerial titles have been earned or bestowed (honorary) on male ministers for many years. Why do you think it is so hard for some to address female clergy in the same? List in detail why this courtesy is so difficult.

_____

_____

_____

_____

_____

_____

_____

_____

4. In your own words, explain what is meant by a "servant's heart." Can you identify with having a servant's heart?

_____

_____

_____

_____

_____

_____

_____

_____

_____

_____

_____

CHAPTER 8

HANDLING CRITICISM AND OPPOSITION WITH GRACE

"Listen to advice and accept instruction,
and in the end, you will be wise"
—Proverbs 19:20 (NIV).

I married and had a child very early in my life, with most of my education ahead of me. Some family members, friends, and associates thought I would never make it or fit into the academic world.

Starting with a Paul D. Camp Community College (now Camp Community College) certificate led me to strive for higher heights in my educational journey. Many said I was delusional in trying for a college certificate, much less associate and baccalaureate degrees. Some did not believe I was going to school at all! This negative feedback from some family members and friends only strengthened my resolve and desire to continue my quest to get as much education as possible to get on a good career path. Instead of becoming discouraged, I used people's criticism to motivate me to do bigger and better things in life.

I advise young women and men not to let nay-sayers stop your progress. Many family members and friends in our culture still cannot see further than a steady job and starting a family. Remember, this is your life. At the end of the day, you are rewarded for what you do, not what other folks think you should be doing. Starting a family too early in life can be a deal breaker for success— for many in terms of moving forward. This is a huge obstacle to overcome, but with the help of God, you can do it. NOT EASILY DONE! You can do it. Keep this phrase in mind: "You Can Do It!"

Criticism – Ministry

I was licensed to preach at Mineral Spring Baptist Church in 1984 under the leadership of the late Rev. George A Speight, Sr. That was a very trying, turbulent, confusing, rewarding, and blessed time in my life. You may ask how entering the ministry could be all these things. Well, I'm glad you did.

I will start with my family. Many still did not believe in me or the goals that God had shown me for my life. The nay-sayers were still there. Now, they have been turned into doubters. Many thought that I just wanted, in their opinion, to "Be Somebody." Our culture does not often handle family members' success well. Ministry seems to be at the top of the list when questioning our journey up and out of the family norm. Many questions, comments, and opinions were thrown at me. To God be the Glory!

Having a husband who was not 100% on board with my next step in life was not much help either. He wanted a "traditional wife" and had some "growing" to do to accept and embrace my calling fully. Things were challenging with some negative people and a mate at home who was not all-in on my quest. Spending so much time on my studies was taking its toll on my personal and family life in a big way. With God and those few who believed in me, I kept praying and pushing.

After being licensed in my home church, I did women's days, special events, and pulpit supply. This allowed me to sharpen my preaching skills somewhat.

Life was still a struggle, and the criticism kept on coming. After I completed my undergraduate degree, I earned a Master's in Education. From there, I pursued a Master of Divinity from the Samuel DeWitt Proctor School of Theology in Richmond, Virginia.

During those days, I was working in administration. I served as an adjunct instructor at Camp College, looking after my family and husband, making hospital visits, and trying to support our broader church activities.

Some of the things that I encountered along the way will make you laugh/cry and sometimes downright angry, but remember, this was the 80s. I was invited to preach in churches that would not allow me to enter the pulpit. Frequently, I had to vest in the choir room, kitchen area, or the corner of a Sunday school classroom. Occasionally, I would think-ok-you can change anywhere in the church, but don't contaminate the pastor's office. I have come across some jealous pastors' wives. Even male pastors who were single seemed to have negative vibes and thoughts in their minds. I often saw and heard things that would make me question their calling. However, I never dwelled on those negative attitudes and the little innuendos. I ignored them, kept praying, and moved forward as the Lord would allow me. I was fine as long as no one would put their hands on me. I knew that God had called and equipped me for the journey, which was sufficient.

My journey would be going smoothly, but something else would happen to unsettled me all over again. Prayer became my best friend because that was the only way I could see my way through trying situations.

Several years ago, I delivered a message at a Youth Conference. It was my first time speaking at a Youth Conference. The youth were ecstatic, partly because it was snowing that Sunday, and everyone was hyped. I was wondering if they would ever calm down. The church leaders and parents were able to get them collected and quiet. We went on and had service, which went very well. When it was over, I was so thankful to God and proud of myself because I thought I had done a great job. I stood around the church's chancel, greeting people as they approached me. I noticed a little boy, who appeared to be around eight years of age, standing nearby, waiting to speak to me. A gentleman stood behind the little boy and told him, "You can go now." The little boy approached me and said, "Ma'am, you did a good job, but your sermon could have been a little longer." I was so disappointed, for the child's statement had shaken my confidence. As I looked up, the father was staring straight into my face. I said the words were "out of the mouth of a babe," but they could have come from his father.

Nonetheless, it took me a while to regain my confidence. I received spiritual support from my pastor and a mother figure in my home church. They helped me immensely. That negative experience enabled me to grow as a young minister. Thanks be to God!

The Call to the Church—The Ultimate Criticism

In 1987, I was called to a neighborhood church in Suffolk, Virginia. The United Church of Christ had written the church off as one without any chance of survival. The congregation had scattered, and the building was in inferior condition. Seemingly, there was no hope left regarding being restored—the building or the membership.

I was visited by two deacons (father and son) to come and help them out. I agreed to go over and help them, and five months later, they installed me as pastor. I began to seek out estranged members, family, friends, and anyone willing to help revive the church. I preached there for several years without an actual salary. Once I located some of the church records, I started contacting people—some started returning while others had connected with another church. And it was encouraging when new folks showed up. Over a reasonable period, we were up and conducting worship services and business meetings, and eventually, we added Bible study. I added other ministries along the way.

Still, there were building issues that needed to be addressed. We later installed more restrooms, communication system/cooling system, and restored a faulty water system. They were just the fundamental issues in the beginning. Later, we replaced floors, roof, windows, sound/media system, and an Annex, including a fellowship hall, offices, and an extra restroom.

A strong criticism was laid on me while our church was making the upgrades mentioned in the last paragraph. One Sunday afternoon, we had a special program at the church. The service was a blessing to all who came, at least I thought it was. At the end of the program, I was greeting people as I always do when an elderly lady walked up to me and said rather pointedly, "Why don't you have a restroom in this place for people like me who have to use canes and walkers?" [I had extended my hand to shake hers, but she never reciprocated.]

I was stunned because she was so bold. She had an angry-looking face. I said, "Ma'am, I am so sorry for not having an accessible restroom. I apologize for the inconvenience that we have caused you." She continued to fuss at me and complained. One of the trustees heard her complaining and came over to see what the problem was.

The disgruntled lady repeated herself. The trustee told her, "Well, Ma'am, please don't blame our pastor for what we don't have; we are renovating our restroom to be equipped for disabled people." He continued apologizing, and so did I. Still mouthing, the lady left the church. Thank God, the trustee, and I both were able to keep a smile on our faces. I was broken for several weeks because of that lady's criticism. But as always, I gave my hurt to the Lord in prayer. The lesson that came out of the elderly lady's criticism and our embarrassment was that the Trustee Ministry became more focused on getting the restroom upgraded and completed according to the handicap regulations.

When someone criticizes you, I will offer the following advice:

1) Maintain your composure.

2) Wear a pleasant face.

3) Apologize.

4) Listen to what the person is saying.

5) Express empathy. Ask if you can be of further assistance to them. Finally, apologize if necessary, again.

To summarize, I realize that criticism can be hurtful at times and it is inevitable. No matter what your family status is, what income bracket you fall in, or what geographical location you live in, someone will criticize you during your lifetime.

It would be best if you learned to work through criticism. The following ways should help you cope with criticism:

➢ Always pray and study God's Word.

➢ Understand yourself, your purpose, and your goals in life.

➢ Look in the mirror; examine yourself.

➢ Put yourself in that person's place.

➢ Important. While not all criticism is constructive, you can learn and grow from constructive and often destructive criticism.

➢ Reflect on any moment of criticism that you have experienced. Ask yourself if you can improve from that same experience in the future.

➢ Always remain prayerful and encourage yourself no matter what.

Remembering the importance of the last seven items should help you turn criticism into opportunities for growth. *Selah.*

Chapter Summary:

- Criticism is inevitable, regardless of one's status or location.

- Learning to handle criticism gracefully is essential for personal and professional growth.

- Turning criticism into opportunities for growth involves self-reflection, empathy, and maintaining a positive attitude.

Self-Reflection:

1. Do you believe that all criticism is good or bad? State your position and explain.

_____

_____

_____

_____

_____

_____

_____

_____

_____

_____

2. As a leader, how would you handle public criticism? Give an example and explain.

_____

_____

_____

_____

_____

_____

_____

_____

_____

_____

3. God has called you into ministry. But there is one problem: your spouse is not on board with it. Would you submit to their wishes? Or do you continue to follow God's plan and try to bring them along? Write down detailed answers.

_____

_____

_____

_____

_____

_____

_____

_____

_____

_____

4. If a person brashly criticized you, how would you respond? Would you get angry? Or would you be calm, listen, and try to understand where the person is coming from?

_____

_____

_____

_____

_____

_____

_____

_____

_____

_____

_____

CHAPTER 9

BALANCING MINISTRY AND PERSONAL LIFE

~~~~~~~~~~

*"For surely I know the plans I have for you, says
the Lord, plans for your welfare and not for harm,
to give you a future with hope"*
–Jeremiah 29:11 (NRSV).

Prioritizing Family and Personal Well-Being

Sisters of the cloth, listen up! Please note that balancing ministry and personal life is probably one of our most challenging situations.

I must confess that time management has been complex for me, especially in the earlier years. I was in school both part-time and full-time. Therefore, it took me longer to finish than most students who were taking classes on a regular track. Also, I worked a 9-5 job, trying to care for my family and do ministry—it was like being on a roller coaster. I was running up and down the road, here and there, trying to keep up with everything. I must tell you that it is impossible to keep up with everything and everybody. Some things will surely fall through the cracks.

I didn't always have the support system that I have today. In retrospect, life was hard for me as I juggled between caring for my kids and spouse and helping to look after my husband's grandparents. I started school, and my husband's grandmother was helping to take care of the kids, but she became ill shortly after I returned to school. That was another setback, not only for me but for the entire family. It was grief and stress all combined. But my husband and I decided on a plan. Hindsight—we missed one important thing; we left God out of the conversation.

I returned to school, and my husband cared for the children after he got home from work. He was such an excellent support system for me, but I could tell that he was getting tired. I would go to school, come home, and take a power nap to get up and study again. To make life more complicated, I wanted to go to a university for a four-year degree after I graduated and received my certificate. I was digging a deeper hole in our relationship. That caused a lot of tension between me and my husband. You might say, that's when all hell broke loose. I was stubborn and selfish, doing what I wanted without consulting him at this juncture. I was feeling nobody's pain but my own. My decisions and actions compounded the stress and resentment between us. My husband told me, "You have no time for the family because you are so busy running here and there—trying to achieve the things that you desire until you forget about us." The sound in his voice and the look on his face shocked me into reality. I knew I had to make a positive change to save the beautiful family God had blessed me with.

I remembered that I had not invited God into our mess. So, I did as I should have in the first place. I turned to God, praying and asking for forgiveness because I had omitted him, my Savior and Mainstay. Immediately, I started reading God's Word, allowing it to saturate my soul. I was so ashamed that I had overlooked Him. My mind wandered to a lofty plane, reflecting on all God had done for me.

I was inspired by Jeremiah 29: 11 "For surely I know the plans I have for you, says the Lord, plans for your welfare and not for harm, to give you a future with hope." Within this text, I felt the power of God's concern for me and my family's situation. I believe He did not want to see our family unit suffer because of my quest to do what I wanted. As I continued to read,

I realized God wanted a future for us [our family]. Not only here on earth, but to hope in God because He is the master planner of everything.

Ladies, as a strong, career-oriented wife, mother, and minister, I had to learn the following principles of real life to save my family. Therefore, I am sharing them to encourage you to reflect on yourself and your approach to planning with and for your family.

1. God is the head of my life.
2. My family comes first.
3. As a married woman, I had to make decisions with my husband and not alone.
4. I had to consider the needs of my children and my husband.
5. I had to learn to be more accountable and responsible.
6. I had to balance my personal life and consider my family's needs.

Improvement Since the Early Days of Ministry

I am better now than I was as a student and new Pastor. As noted previously, I faced many challenges as a young woman who had not reached her desired goals in life.

But as time passed, I learned, with the help of God and the church and community elders, that I needed to consider my well-being. After becoming a minister and Pastor of a church, I shifted the attention from myself to putting everyone else's wants and needs ahead of mine and sometimes my family. However, I realized that my first ministry was my family. Let me pause and say that God is first in my life. Once I understood that and embraced the fact that my family was my responsibility, life has been so much better.

As a young minister, I experienced the "Messiah Syndrome," which means I couldn't say "no" to other people's requests. Whether I felt sick or was concerned about what was going on with my family, I always tried to respond positively to every request. If I were asked to visit the sick, attend a funeral service, or a special event. Every time I was called upon, I went!

The harsh reality is that most people do not consider your family or personal well-being. They want what they want done. I soon learned that I was running myself into poor health—mentally and physically—as I tried to keep up the pace of being there for everyone else and their situations. My family was also being neglected. (Very well Mind. https://www.verywellmind.com/savior-complex-8357155).

Today, I can genuinely say that I have learned to consider my well-being by evaluating the situation and prioritizing from the most important to the least. I also learned the power of saying, "No!" which was unbelievable. There have been times that I was asked to preach or attend a community event, but if the time was not suitable for my well-being, I declined. I really had to adapt to saying "No," though.

As a Pastor and person, I am healthier and wiser because of praying. I make decisions now that allow me to take care of myself. This allows me to take care of others better; others, such as family, community and the church.

COVID-19 Led to New Ways for Doing Ministry

I had to learn to do ministry in new ways when COVID came. That deadly virus really shocked me in so many ways, especially trying to continue to provide ministry and pastoral care to members and friends of my congregation. After the CDC placed restrictions on the public and we had to shelter in place for several months, it was the worst for me because I believe in touching and agreeing and visiting the sick. I knew that I had to do something since I was not able to visit the sick members in their homes, hospitals, nursing facilities, or rehab centers.

I prayed earnestly and leaned on God to inspire me to embrace ideas and new ministry methods. God was my helper; He was my way maker.

One of my parishioners was terminally ill and was not expected to live much longer. I asked God to I asked God to give me an idea, show me a sign, or anything that would help me to reach and minister to this person. One day, the celestial light came on, and I was given the idea and vision of creating a lovely gift box covered with butterflies. The box included the following items: a get-well card, throw, neck scarf, footies, a candy cane card with a story, a meditation booklet, a handwritten prayer, and a communion packet. I contacted someone in the home, asking them if they would meet me at the door.

They replied, "Yes, ma'am." Upon arrival, I gave the lovely box to a relative who greeted me on the stoop. I spoke to her as I stood outside. I didn't keep her long because she was not only sick but weak. She was grateful and deeply moved. Later, I heard she talked about the Pastor bringing her a nice box for months. The parishioner lived about six months longer than the doctors expected. God, indeed, still works miracles.

Thus, COVID-19 taught me a new concept of pastoral ministry: I now make smaller gift boxes to give to individuals in person or shut-in.

During COVID, we were forced to use different worship approaches to our services, Bible study, Sunday school, and business meetings. It felt strange initially, but we tried drive-in worship, which was not embraced because of the environmental elements.

Most of us didn't know how to use Zoom. So, I organized a team, and we studied diligently for about three weeks until we felt knowledgeable enough to teach and lead others in learning how to use Zoom. We then launched Zoom and used it for all aspects of our church activities. Today, we do hybrid worship, which includes in-person worship, Zoom, and social media.

We needed to keep our giving moving forward. To show you how God works, I saw a demonstration on Givelify approximately two years before the pandemic. God was winking at me then. I thought it would suit the church, so I signed up for the trial, but we didn't upload it to the church's computer until after the pandemic set in. Thank God for Jesus! There we were, ready for the new way of "giving" to the church. Most of the congregants use Givelify today.

We had to change our approach to administering the Lord's Supper from the traditional method to packaging and distributing individually to help prevent them from possibly getting the Coronavirus. This was a deal breaker because I am still trying to adapt to this new concept.

I assigned parish leaders to the church's "groups of members" during COVID-19. Thank God that was a powerful and productive move because the parish leaders were able to keep not only me informed but also everyone informed and connected during the worst part of the pandemic.

Finally, I pray that the experiences and principles I shared in this chapter will help you understand and appreciate the importance of prioritizing family, education, career, well-being, and ministry.

It is paramount that you do not leave God out of your decision-making and life. Remember to "Trust in the Lord with all your heart, and do not rely on your own insight. In all your ways acknowledge him, and he will make straight your paths" (Proverbs 3:5-6 NRSV).

You can also learn new and innovative things from chaotic situations such as the COVID-19 pandemic. So many have asked, "Where was God when all that happened?" Please be encouraged that, according to scripture, God is forever present in all circumstances (Psalm 139 NRSV).

Chapter Summary:

- Balancing Life and Ministry by involving God, prioritizing family, and learning accountability are vital to maintaining a healthy balance.

- Set boundaries and prioritize your well-being, enabling better care for family and ministry.

- Sometimes, you must adapt. During COVID-19, innovations like Zoom worship and gift boxes ensured continued pastoral care.

- Trust God, embrace change, and prioritize your relationships to enhance life and ministry effectiveness.

Self-Reflection:

1. Do you prioritize your family and their needs? Or do you allow everyone to decide based on their wants and needs? If yes, explain. If not, explain.

_____

_____

_____

_____

_____

_____

_____

_____

_____

2. After reading this chapter, what do you conclude "Messiah syndrome" to be? Give an example.

_____

_____

_____

_____

_____

_____

_____

_____

_____

3. Why is it vital to reflect on your life and how you have lived versus today? Describe and list the differences as you reflect.

_____

_____

_____

_____

_____

_____

_____

_____

_____

4. The COVID-19 pandemic caused death, sickness, and permanent side effects for some people. Can you cite any positive changes that surfaced because of it? Based on your experience, write about those positive changes that occurred in your life or in someone else's life that you know.

_____

_____

_____

_____

_____

_____

_____

_____

_____

CHAPTER 10

CULTIVATING A SPIRIT OF PRAYER

"The fervent prayer of a righteous person is very powerful" –James 5:16b, (NABRE).

I was raised and nurtured in a praying home and community. Prayers and blessings over the meals were offered in the church, at special events, and at school. The community in which we lived was composed mainly of families who farmed. I witnessed and heard prayers cited during planting season and harvest time by many. It was amazing to me that after the saints prayed, God blessed their harvest time. While it was not always abundant, they were thankful God answered their prayers. I was a young child, but I was sensitive to their prayers and happy for the joy they received from God's blessings.

My maternal Grandma, Lily Mae, cultivated a spirit of prayer within me by teaching me to pray. She introduced me to prayer when I was a toddler—

three or four. I could speak well but was not able to read at that time. Grandma often cited words to me to pray until I became old enough to say more advanced prayers. She would tell me, "Now baby, pray for your mama and your daddy, brothers and sisters, and all the people in this community, and—don't forget your grandma and granddaddy, Amen." And, of course, I would say every prayer statement she repeated to me. I smiled when I finished saying my prayers and was so proud of myself. Saying my prayers always warmed me.

Then Grandma graduated me to the following prayer:

"Now I lay me down to sleep,

I pray thee Lord my soul to keep;

For if I die before I wake,

I pray thee Lord my soul to take.

Amen."

This prayer was a little challenging for me to learn, but by the time my grandmother finished drilling it in my head, I had memorized it. She would randomly call on me to recite the prayer until I learned it with meaning.

As mentioned earlier in this book, my grandmother taught me prayers, Psalm 23, the Pledge Alliance, and numerals 1-50, all before I started school.

I was six or seven years of age when I learned to pray the Lord's model prayer. It took me a little longer to learn this prayer. I thank God daily for my late grandmother, Lillie Mae because she was my prayer warrior. She instilled and cultivated a spirit of prayer in me.

The Power of Prayer in Leadership

Having been nurtured in prayer, I have experienced the power of prayer in many different spiritual aspects. First, to appreciate prayer, you must know what it means. Prayer is communicating with God. It is equally important to note that everyone, as they wish, can pray to their God. He [God] welcomes our prayers when our hearts are faithful, humble, and sincere.

As stated, there is a collage of powerful aspects to prayer. These aspects can transform and allow us to have a stronger relationship with God. For this writing, I will introduce four elements of the power of prayer that I have found consolation in.

The first aspect of the power of prayer is found in my *direct relationship with God* through His birth, death, and resurrection. I do not need to go to a confession booth to talk to a priest. I can intimately communicate with God about my problems and shortcomings. When I ask God for forgiveness, based on the word, I believe Jesus forgives me. As a result, I feel transformed and relieved of my burdens. Thus, my spirit is refreshed, my mental facilities are clear, and I am free to be all God would have me to be.

Second, I find *strength* in the power of prayer. As a servant leader, I pray for strength daily to help me carry out God's plans for my family, Christ's church, and the community.

I am not complaining, but being an administrator [senior pastor], preparing sermons, participating in the teaching ministry, supporting the spiritual needs of the congregants, and participating in the wider community drain me mentally and physically. I go to God in prayer, asking Him for strength and wisdom so that I can move forward. When I become mentally and physically tired, I read the following scripture from Isaiah 40: 29-31, NIV:

"He gives strength to the weary and increases the power of the weak.

Even youths grow tired and weary, and young men stumble and fall;

but those who hope in the Lord will renew their
strength. They will soar on wings like eagles;
they will run and not grow weary,
They will walk and not be faint."

This scripture not only boosts my strength, but it was encouraging as well.

My third aspect of the power of prayer is *confidence*. Through prayer, God always gives the spirit of faith. When I was young in the ministry, I prayed constantly for God's power to anoint me with conviction because I felt inadequate. As a female minister, it seemed like everyone else was satisfied with the level of ministry they had achieved. Some bragged about what they were doing in ministry, their church affiliations, or their Alma Mater. I was so bothered by this until I shared my thoughts and feelings regarding my lack of confidence with a senior minister several times.

He told me not to worry about what somebody else was saying because they do not have all they claim to have half of the time. Amazingly, his words panned out to be true. And if they did, so what? He encouraged me not to worry because God was equipping me slowly so that I would be a good minister for

His vineyard. The minister drew my attention to one of Paul's epistles, 2 Corinthians 12:9 NIV, but he said to me, "My grace is sufficient for you, for my power is made perfect in weakness." After this, he, the minister, anointed and prayed for me, I was refreshed from on high. Praise God!

Since the early days of my ministry, I have cited that scripture many times. Although I have many years under my belt, am well educated, have lots of experience, and have been blessed with much wisdom from God, my confidence is sometimes still shaken. Hence, I remind myself, "That His grace is sufficient for me..." God maintains my confidence with His power through my fervent and selfless prayers.

My fourth and last aspect of the power of prayer is *boldness*. The following scripture was my bridge to boldness. "Be strong and courageous. Do not fear or dread them, for it is the Lord your God who goes with you. He will not leave you or forsake you" (Deuteronomy 31:6 NIV). My dear clergy sisters, you wouldn't believe how shy and timid I was around people in my early 30s. During one fall revival, I was sitting on the back pew in the church when God called me out, and I floated to the altar. You see, I was hiding because I didn't have the boldness to be amid people. I was not particularly eager to talk and didn't want to mingle with people, but I love them dearly.

After God called me from the pews to serve Him wholly and solely, He equipped me for the journey. [I hadn't received the call to the ministry during this time.] God gave me the utterance and boldness to converse with people, and He conditioned me to help heal the sick through the power of prayer. I was faithful, and God never failed me.

Therefore, prayer is essential to leaders. Based on my life experiences and as a pastor, I cannot lead without prayer. I can't even imagine life without prayer. Knowing I have a God to communicate with in good and bad times gives me a strong sense of security. I know I can pray to God when no one else is available or trustworthy.

Jesus Christ, the head of our lives, was an excellent role model of prayer. As recorded in Matthew 6: 5-13, the New Kings James Version, Jesus discussed prayer with his disciples, sharing His model of prayer affirmations with them. Jesus was concerned about the disciples praying fervently [sincerely] from their hearts. He made it clear that they should not pray as hypocrites. Their prayers were showy and in public, not sincere, and filled with vain repetitions. In verse

8, Jesus said, "Therefore do not be like them. Your Father knows the things you need before you ask Him." In essence, Jesus wanted his disciples to humbly and fervently pray to God for the forgiveness of self and others, deliverance, and encouragement.

Here is Jesus' model prayer from the King James Translation. It has helped to transform many souls in this world. Pray it with me –

9"Our Father which art in heaven, Hallowed be thy name.

10Thy kingdom come. Thy will be done in earth, as it is in heaven.

11Give us this day our daily bread.

12 And forgive us our debts, as we forgive our debtors.

13And lead us not into temptation, but deliver us from evil:

For thine is the kingdom, and the power, and the glory, forever.

Amen."

If you are a Christian believer, you know that Jesus has established and strongly cultivated a spirit of prayer in his life, his disciples, and ours.

Developing a Personal Prayer Life

Developing a strong personal prayer life is one of the best things you can do for your spiritual growth. I admit that you cannot thrust yourself into creating a powerful prayer life all in an instant. It takes time, spiritual maturity, faith, patience, Bible study, and other resources to discuss and delve more deeply into the framework of prayer. As I have realized, prayers with the best results in life are cultivated with a sincere and faithful heart. The more you practice praying, the more natural it becomes.

I expanded my prayer life by studying biblical characters known for their prayers, listening to others pray, reading other books on prayer, and being a good prayer partner.

In addition to Christ's model of prayer, I have used the ACTS by Marybeth Wuenschel. Listed below is the acronym for the model:

A—Adoration: Give God praise
C—Confession: Ask for forgiveness
T—Thanksgiving: Thank God
S—Supplication: Make your request known

The acronym will help you develop a prayer from your heart that will put your thoughts and words into perspective when praying. Accordingly, there are many types/divisions of prayers depending on your needs. Some religious adherents do not believe in writing their prayers because they feel it's not from the heart. I beg them to differ. I used to have that same mindset, but I realized years ago that as I wrote my prayers, the words came from my heart and soul.

Seeking God's Guidance Through Prayer

It is a must to seek God through prayer. I recall many times when I didn't seek God first, at various times in my life. I hope you remember reading a previous chapter about my husband and me trying to develop a plan to care for our children while I was attending college. Let me remind you again: I almost lost my husband because I was so set in my ways and had to do everything my way. Thank God there was a moment when we stopped, prayed, and continued with our discussion. It all turned out well because we leaned and depended on God for everything from that moment on. So, as a word of caution, remember you can't do life without seeking God's guidance first.

I have had many unanswered prayers during my lifetime, though. Perhaps some people would say unanswered prayers mean your heart is not sincere about God or His matters. But centered on my experiences, I feel that when God doesn't answer our prayers, it could be because we are spiritually insufficient—lacking wisdom, impatience, or humility. Ultimately, some of my prayer requests were unanswered at the time because God was not ready, or He had not destined them to come to fruition for me yet.

Personal Experiences

I was born into a culture whereby the family and community prayed without written prayers. Of course, the pastors and congregations where I was nurtured in Christ didn't really write prayers. Seldom did I see anyone reading prayers. All of that changed after I received the call to the ministry. I expressed concern to my pastor about being nervous when praying in public, and he told me to write my prayers until I became comfortable with praying in public. Pastor told me I was a good prayer warrior but thought I had a little stage fright. As noted, my pastor was always encouraging.

Currently, my prayer rituals consist of praying three times a day. I also pray sentence prayers throughout the day. I do meditations twice daily: a short one in the morning to get me started for the day and another around 10:30 p.m. The latter prayer and meditation last approximately 45 minutes to an hour. I may also lay prostrate on the floor, praying and waiting to hear a word from God. Also, as the Holy Spirit leads me, I will fast and pray. Depending on my spiritual needs, I might light a candle and remain "still" and silent. Psalm 46:10a (NIV) says, "Be still, and know that I am God."

As a seasoned minister, I know it is still good to write prayers. Written prayers can help to keep me focused on the purpose of the prayer if I am having a hectic time. Recently, I have been reading books on how to pray to the scriptures. This is a powerful and effective method of praying because you are using God's words to formulate your prayers.

Listed are three different divisions of prayers that I have written for this chapter:

Prayer #1: Discouragement

Our Father, which art in heaven. I praise and thank you for giving us your only Son, Jesus Christ. God, I know I have sinned and come short of your Glory. Please forgive me for the sins that I have committed and those whom I have trespassed against. I am thankful for my health, strength, and family. But Lord, I feel discouraged right now due to the state of our government. Hear my prayer, O Lord, and heal our nation. Please grant my prayer request, all in the name of the Father, the Son, and the Holy Spirit. Amen.

Prayer #2: Marriage

O Lord, our God, I praise you from whom all blessings flow. I confess my faults and sins to you. I pray for the couples who are married, starting together with different views and opinions. Dear Lord, I pray they will make you the head of their lives. Fill them with your love and wisdom. Entreat them not to leave thee. I bless and thank you, Lord, for the great things you have done in our lives and will do in the future. I pray that married couples will bring all their supplications to you and that you will answer their prayers according to your will. In the mighty name of Jesus Christ, I pray, Amen.

Prayer #3: Our Children and Youth

Dear Lord Jesus, we are so grateful that God, our Father, sent you to save us from our sins. I am humbled and thankful for the abundance you have given us. As a minister and parent, I pray for the welfare of our children and youth. Because they live in a world of abuse, violence, human trafficking, and hatred, I am asking that you watch over them and protect them from day to day. Help our children know the difference between right and wrong. I pray that their parents will be wiser teachers and provide better protection for their children. Thank you, God, for answering my prayer requests. In the name of the Father, Son, and Holy Spirit. Amen.

To Conclude

Leading ladies, if by chance you didn't grow up in an environment of prayer, cultivate one for you and your family. Then, saturate yourself in prayer. Prayer is not an option—it is REQUIRED. It is the key to God's kingdom. You must stand in the gap, praying for your families, church, communities, and the nation.

As indicated earlier, those in leadership roles must lead with the power of prayer. We must trust God and lean not to our understanding. In our communion with God, we find intimacy, strength, confidence, boldness, and wisdom for the journey.

Establishing a schedule for prayer and meditation will nurture and feed your spirituality. Staying in prayer will help you cope better with the wiles of Satan and the struggles of life. Satan will try to block your blessings by attacking your prayer life. When you have made prayer requests to God and your prayers seem to remain unanswered, call the devil a liar. I charge you to keep praying because God will answer your prayer in his way and in due season. Amen.

Chapter Summary:

- Being raised in a prayerful home helps nurture a prayer life, starting with simple prayers and progressing from there.

- Prayer strengthens leadership by fostering a relationship with God, building confidence, boldness, and resilience, supported by scripture.

- Cultivate prayer through consistency, biblical examples, the ACTS method, and reflective practices like writing prayers.

- Prayer is important for clarity and peace, recognizing unanswered prayers as part of God's timing and wisdom.

Self-Reflection:

1. Prayer is a powerful tool because you can communicate directly to God anytime. Do you recall your first prayer experience? If so, try to remember the words. If you can, explain your feelings and mental attitude during prayer.

_____

_____

_____

_____

_____

_____

_____

_____

2. What tools would you use to help expand your personal prayer life? List and discuss them.

_____

_____

_____

_____

_____

_____

_____

_____

3. What is the difference between Jesus' model prayer-- the Lord's Prayer-- and the prayer given in John 17:1-25?

_____

_____

_____

_____

_____

_____

_____

_____

4. Whether you are a beginner or a seasoned person of prayer, you should pray with purpose. What steps would you take to pray with purpose and organization? State the tools or model you would use and list the steps for creating your prayer.

_____

_____

_____

_____

_____

_____

_____

_____

CHAPTER 11

LEADING WITH LOVE

"And so we know and rely on the love God has for us. God is love. Whoever lives in love lives in God, and God in them" –1 John 4:16 (NIV).

Leading with love can have two different dichotomies. The idea is leading with GODLY LOVE, as demonstrated by our Lord and Savior, Jesus Christ. God's love is pure, authentic, sound, and unconditional. However, as life would have it, there is always the opposite of leading with God's love. Leading without God's love can be summed up as vague, obscure, conditional, and illusive by people with ulterior motives and agendas.

Walking among humanity are those who will do anything and everything in the name of love. They say they love us, but they really do not love us or *lead* with love as Christ would. Instead of leading with genuine love or Agape love, they lead with hidden agendas—meaning their plans for others are often masked or veiled, if you would. At this juncture, I will unveil the actions and attitudes of love that some have no idea is as phony and conditional as can be.

Women of God, you must know what's behind the veil when leading and building relationships. By the way, I am not talking about the wedding veil either. The promises, hidden agendas, and desperation about things you want to achieve can be treacherous to your spiritual welfare and the development of your ministry. Listen and watch out for them! Therefore, you must continue to pray and watch for the unforeseen ills of people.

Building Strong Relationships Within Your Ministry

Let us look at what is behind the veil of obscurity. The hard realization of building relationships in ministry is due to being blinded and deafened by cunning conversations and underhanded actions by some leaders.

At the outset of my ministry, I was the "new kid on the block," as they say, with very few women pastors or ministers to seek advice. It was a task to get support and guidance from my male counterparts. Being a young female, I had to choose wisely and carefully those individuals from whom I sought confidence and advice. Building strong relationships can be tricky when most people in your field are of the opposite gender. So, building strong relationships became sort of a minefield.

A strong relationship in ministry or any field requires letting another person in your personal space. I found that everyone who threw out a welcoming lifeline was not sincere. This issue can be an obstacle for many female clergy. Our wants and desires can make us vulnerable to abuse and the misuse of power by others.

Thank God I had a wise and supportive pastor to guide and warn me of some pitfalls and wolves dressed in sheep's clothing. My dear clergy sisters, the wolves will test you. Remember, that's part of the veil of obscurity. I learned quickly who and what to stay away from.

My husband also was there to explain the male gender's point of view to me. Conversely, every woman may not have a husband willing, without bias, to inform her of the truth from a man's perspective. If you do not have a supportive husband or a significant other to walk with you, I would suggest that you pray fervently and look for a mentor with a kindred spirit. You can also seek a support group that will give you authentic advice and encouragement while you are trying to establish yourself in ministry during uncertain times, struggles, and unforeseen circumstances.

Building a strong relationship with the right people and organizations became a challenge that God and others helped me to overcome. You cannot do ministry effectively alone. I have seen many of my brothers and sisters try it but to no avail; they weren't successful. As quoted by John Donne, a seventeenth-century author, "No man or woman is an island…" This was interpreted as people needing each other to survive. (allpoetry.com). Thus, ministry entails services to humanity. So, you can't avoid working and serving with other people.

I learned very early who to embrace and stay away from on my ministerial journey. Everybody who tells you they love you "Ain't your friend." And I found this out on a large scale. Choose your friends wisely. Even some big spenders/donors are not always showing up with your interest at heart—it's about them. Sadly, they could have their hidden agendas, too. People with the wrong intentions can make life unbearable in the church, the ministry, and across all facets of your life. Pray hard when someone new shows up in your church that seems perfect for your ministry. THINK: if they are too perfect, then chances are they will not make a good fit for the congregation. Now that I have revealed some of the obscurities of love behind the veil, let's look at what leading with God's authentic love is like in leadership. God's love is not hidden behind a veil of obscurity. It permeates the atmosphere and God's genuine people, whether followers or leaders.

The Transformative Power of Love in Leadership

God's veil of love is like no other; it is transparent. You do not have to guess about His love. Christ's love was so transparent that you can feel it demonstrated throughout God's Holy Scriptures. He never met a stranger, and no matter what social class or economic strata a person was from, Jesus never turned them away.

Another critical aspect of Jesus is that He was cosmopolitan, which meant He met people at their living level. It didn't matter to Jesus where people were from or whose surname they carried. All of these factors encourage me to lead with God's transforming love.

While not all-inclusive, I lead with love and govern my actions by the following scriptures:

- "For God so loved the world that He gave His one and only Son, that whosoever believes in Him shall not perish but have eternal life" (John 3:16 NIV).

- "We love because He first loved us. If anyone says, "I love God," yet hates his brother, he is a liar. For anyone who does not love his brother, whom he has seen, cannot love God, whom he has not seen" (I John 4: 19-20 NIV).

- "Do to others as you would have them do to you" (Luke 6:31 NRSV).

Practicing Compassion and Understanding

I love and honor God so much, and I always wanted to express my love to His people by fashioning myself after Him.

There are so many ways to practice God's love. You must first love yourself to express authentic love to your family and God's people. If I don't love myself, how can I show you love? Love is not just a noun but a verb—it shows action.

I practice compassion and understanding with my family, friends, and church members. Listed are some approaches that I use when leading with love. One word of caution: if I had a large congregation, I probably wouldn't be able to express my love the way I currently do, at least not to the extent that I do, because I wouldn't be able to get around to them all. However, I would devise another method to serve a larger congregation because I am a "people person."

1. I prayerfully and rightly discern the proper approach to whomever I communicate with.

2. Listening is essential when ministering to people.

3. On Sundays, I do not schedule any appointments or counseling sessions because I want to greet and be actively engaged with my parishioners.

4. During fellowship hour, I will move from person to person, hugging them and telling them I love and appreciate them.

5. Children and youth are important to me. Therefore, I give them the same respect I give to adults, except that I communicate on the youth level.

6. If I recognize someone appears to have a problem, I will tell them I will call them in a few days. Or they are welcome to contact me.

7. I also lead with love by sending cards, calling, texting, and emailing.

8. I express love and compassion to people, not only my church members. I visit them and call them as if I were their pastor.

9. When families are going through sickness and death, I always pray with them and tell them I love

them and wish that I could fix the problem. Most of them love to hear me say that. Those few words bring a strong sense of comfort to them.

Personal Experiences

After having so many different experiences in ministry, I saw the need to support other women who feel inspired in ministry. In 2008, I founded Deborah's Women In Ministry (DWIM), Inc. of Greater Hampton Roads, a support group for women aspiring to the ministry. We welcome those who are discerning and licensed and those who are in authorized ministry. We help to affirm, equip, and empower women in ministry. We award scholarships annually to high school students who are deserving. Additionally, we provide services to various organizations in the community. Our love and support go beyond the conference room.

Over the years, many women have joined the organization. Some have left for various reasons. I make a point of telling new members this organization is not for everyone. Therefore, you may not feel the need to remain with the group for long. Some women have short-term needs, while others desire to be lifetime members. But those of us who have stayed have formed a sisterhood of love and support for one another. There is a meeting of the minds to address critical issues we have experienced in the ministry. Sometimes, it's good news, and other times it's indifferent. Our issues range from how we have experienced bias from church leadership to the people in the pews.

We have established strong relationships that support one another, our families, our churches, and the community. We have an open dialogue about issues that concern women in ministry. When we gather, we always pray and share meditations.

As a founder and member of DWIM, I love and appreciate all the ladies who have joined. We are a diverse group; therefore, each person brings their authentic self and gifts to the organization.

I have the most tremendous respect and love for the members of DWIM because they love the Lord and their families. They are accountable and responsible for whatever they commit to doing.

As I end this chapter, I am aware that there are all kinds of people in this world. Some do not govern their life according to God's principles of love in the Bible. But we must try to understand and be able to communicate and show our appreciation to all people as we lead them with love. My philosophy is, "They need leaders who lead with love, too."

Chapter Summary:

- Leading with God's love is pure, authentic, and transparent, unlike the conditional and self-serving love demonstrated by individuals with hidden motives.

- Building relationships in ministry can be difficult due to biases and hidden agendas, requiring women to be discerning, prayerful, and cautious in choosing mentors and allies.

- Practicing God's love involves compassion, listening, and consistent support through personal engagement, communication, and actions like prayer, visits, and outreach.

- The Deborah's Women In Ministry (DWIM) organization supports, equips, and affirms women in ministry, fostering a sisterhood of love and addressing issues like bias while serving the community.

Self-Reflection:

1. People represent with different faces, so how can you detect whether they are sincere in their words, deeds, and actions? Are there some unique characteristics about them that reveal to you who they really are? With your insight, can you tell if they are true or deceptive? Describe in detail what you have experienced down these lines. List the traits that described the type of human being they presented to you.

_____

_____

_____

_____

_____

_____

_____

_____

2. Share with your pastor and leadership team if you feel God is calling on you to do ministry. It is equally essential for you to seek support from others, but be wise. At this reading, do you know someone that would be a good mentor for you? Write their name, position in the church, and how

long they have been in the church and community. Do consider networking, for it is a powerful aid. Also, compose at least five questions that would be helpful to your spiritual development.

_____

_____

_____

_____

_____

_____

_____

_____

_____

3. What is your favorite Scripture about love? Write it and give three reasons why this Scripture is meaningful to you.

_____

_____

_____

_____

_____

_____

_____

_____

4. You may not have been born with strong attributes of love and compassion. If you wanted to develop more in this area, how would you do it?

_____

_____

_____

_____

_____

_____

_____

_____

_____

_____

CONCLUSION: A WORD FROM THE AUTHOR

I have read many genres of books and devotionals, but this book has enabled me to see myself the most. The abundant presence of God is seen and felt all through these pages. This literary work has allowed me to check and challenge myself and, yes, slow my pace of life and give way to the beauty of God's tapestry.

I have gained wisdom that assisted me with ministry, family life, dealing with difficult people, balancing my personal life, and seeking a more vigorous prayer life. I have learned that some things were not in God's plan for me. And I needed not to force God's hand to make things happen; otherwise, something else would become broken. One principal rationale about life is that you can only do so much.

I am living in answered prayers. God grounded me and enlarged my territory. In addition to being a pastor, God blessed me with powerful preaching opportunities—revivals, conferences, and special events that I had never dreamed of doing. I have had the privilege to travel and speak in other countries, including Mars Hill, Athens, Greece, where the Apostle Paul spoke.

At one time, I was a "wanna be" but by HIS GRACE, I am living in answered prayers. He has given me the desires of my heart. I have also been elevated to other positions in the broader church that I never fathomed.

Answered prayers—God fulfilled my life's dream by allowing me to start writing. I co-authored "Words of Wisdom for the Heart and Soul, Volume III—" Empowered by Cathy Staton. The name of my chapter was "The Call to Lead."

This book has been a blessing to pen. It's like flying at an altitude just high enough for you to look down and visibly see the plans and designs that God had for your life while allowing you to be your authentic self.

I am humbled and grateful to God that I can be a source of support and encouragement to leading ladies of the ministry.

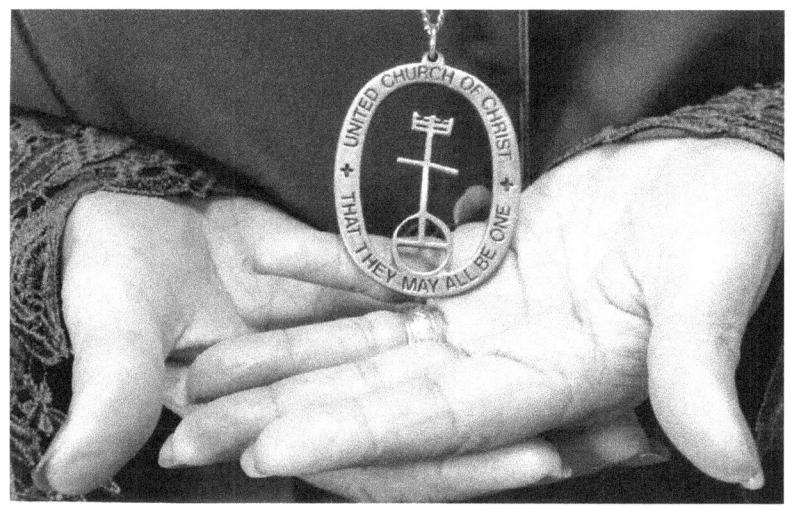

Encouragement for Continued Growth: Next Steps

Clergy sisters, if God didn't call you to pastor a church, it is not for you. So, stop destroying yourselves and your family by trying to "force" a call to happen. I am not saying that God will never call you, but you must listen to His voice and the leading of the Holy Spirit. Do not allow others to push you into the ministry or anything else. Ladies, God's got your plan covered. "For I know the plans I have for you, declares the Lord, plans to prosper you and not to harm you, plans to give you hope and a future" (Jeremiah 29:11 NIV).

As I look back, the one thing I would have done differently was to spend more quality time with my family rather than being so driven and task-oriented. While I achieved most of the things I wanted, it put a strain on my family at the time. In addition to the gift of eternal life, your family is the most important gift God can give you, so spend quality time with them. When your schedule is tight and hectic, plan time with your family. I promise you'll regret it if you don't take my advice. Time is one thing that we cannot dial back.

I still struggle to make time for self-care. Because of my temperament, I am energetic and do not like being still for a long time. Take a note from me and schedule some "me time." During this time, do your favorite hobby or craft, go shopping, take short trips, or walk on a nature trail or park. Prayer and meditation are always excellent practices during self-care.

Closing Prayer for Leading Ladies of Faith

"Unto thee, O God, do we give thanks, unto thee do we give thanks: for that thy name is near thy wondrous works declare." I praise you for being our awesome God.

You declared the world into being. You created us and gave life to us. All of us have sinned and come short of your glory. So, we ask forgiveness for our many sins and trespasses. As leading ladies of faith, help us to be sensitive to the needs of our families and others who cross our paths. Please help us to be better spouses, ministers, leaders, teachers, mentors, mothers, grandmothers, and neighbors.

Lord, I intercede on behalf of our leading ladies of faith to seek your direction for those reading this book, which was written for guidance and encouragement along life's journey. Let us look to God for our elevations in ministry and His plans for us.

As women of God, let us be reminded that we are your children and must live our lives accordingly. As we continue to seek your face, may the word, "Be a lamp unto my feet, and a light unto my pathway." Be not only listeners of Thy word but doers of Thy word.

Heavenly Father, thank you for wisdom, knowledge, love, healing, restored health, and strength. I am grateful for the abundant blessings you have bestowed on us all. If we had ten thousand tongues, we couldn't thank you enough.

God, you have heard my prayers and supplications. Please grant them in the name of the Father, Son, and Holy Spirit. Amen

ACKNOWLEDGMENTS

First, I would like to thank God for allowing me to write this book. It has been in my spirit from the beginning of my ministry. God imbued me with many experiences so that I could be a supporter and mentor to other women who are either already in ministry or inspiring and aspiring.

My deepest gratitude is to my beloved husband, Arnold, for supporting me through the years, especially this writing initiative. He has always encouraged me in my journey from the very inception of it all.

With special acknowledgments to our immediate family: daughter—Savarna (George), son—Arnold, Jr. (Cheryl), grandchildren Arielle and Chanta' (Leighton), and great-grandchildren for being a part of my life and legacy. I hope you will be inspired by my story and someday share your own.

I appreciate the support of my sisters Shirley F. Williams, Rose F. Boone, Irene Flood, and my sister-in-love, Patricia E. Burdell, and other family members who have supported me over the years of my ministry.

I am grateful to my immediate support team: Nakisha T. White, Jacqueline A. Cargill, Rev. Dr. Ann W. Hill, Rose F. Boone, Arnold H. Beard, Sr., and Tamakia S. Hamlin. They are oftentimes burdened to keep me going as they lovingly support me with whatever I need to keep moving forward with my book signings, promotional items, technical support, creative designs, and travel.

Then, there is the Galatians United Church of Christ (GUCC), where God moved so much that they called me to be their pastor. I will be eternally grateful for the "call" and the love GUCC has shown me for 38 years. They helped me to grow and develop as a young pastor, without criticism but with love and kindness, into a seasoned pastor.

I sincerely appreciate Dr. Edward S. Davis, Dr. John T. Myers, Dr. Ann W. Hill, Dr. Veronica R. Coleman, and Dr. Jerome O. Lee for their remarkable contributions to my book. I also extend a heartfelt thank you to the anonymous ministers who provided their personal case studies, which serve as experiential verbatims to readers who may encounter similar experiences.

Words of gratitude to Hope Sheree Stith, who gave me a copy of Words of Wisdom for the Heart and

Soul, Volume II. While reading the book, I realized I was at a pivotal point. I knew it was time to share my story. The saga got even better, and I registered with Visionary Cathy Staton's "Words of Wisdom for the Heart and Soul, Volume III" writing group. I shall never forget this valuable experience, and to that end, I became one of the co-authors of that book. I must mention what my granddaughter, Arielle Nelson and nephew, Elliot Boone Sr., said after I was published in the anthology. They were miles apart, yet they both had the foresight to see that I could write a whole book. They both at separate times congratulated me, and said, "You should write your own book." I had thought of it, but that was further confirmation. Thus, I decided to write a book.

After this, I had the opportunity to meet Coach Tara Tucker—a publisher—who, with her expertise, faith, and patience, has helped me fulfill the dream of writing this book that I have had in my spirit for many years and for that, I will always be eternally grateful.

Finally, I will not continue to call names because the list is too long. However, I want to thank God for all the people who have poured into me from childhood until now. Thanks be to God!

ABOUT THE AUTHOR

Reverend Dr. Madelene F. Beard has faithfully served as the pastor of Galatians United Church of Christ in Suffolk, VA, for an impressive 38 years.

Her educational journey is marked by dedication and achievement. Dr. Beard holds a certificate in Steno-clerical Arts from Paul D. Camp Community College (now Camp Community College) in Franklin, VA, and a B.S. in Administrative Systems from Norfolk State University. Her quest for knowledge continued with an M.Ed. from Virginia State University and an M.Div. from Samuel DeWitt Proctor School of Theology in Richmond, VA. Notably, she earned a D. Min. from Virginia University of Lynchburg (VUL), where her dissertation, "How to Encourage Members of a Congregation to Tithe According to Biblical

Principles," has been instrumental in her church's growth.

Beyond her academic pursuits, Dr. Beard completed the School of Clinical Pastoral Education (CPE) at Sentara Norfolk General Hospital. Her diverse career includes roles in administration, banking, and mortgage lending, as well as teaching in both public schools and the Paul D. Camp Community College System (now Camp Community College). She also shared her knowledge by teaching Biblical Studies at VUL's Suffolk Site, using her academic achievements to further the cause of kingdom-building.

In addition to her pastoral duties, Dr. Beard is the esteemed President and Founder of Deborah's Women In Ministry of Greater Hampton Roads, Inc. She is an active member of Epsilon Theta Zeta Chapter, Zeta Phi Beta Sorority, Inc., where she serves as the chaplain and received the esteemed 2020 Zeta of the Year Award.

Dr. Beard has served in many volunteer positions in the Southern Conference and Eastern Virginia Association (EVA) of the United Church of Christ. She teaches "Boundary Training" and facilitates workshops upon request. Beard is a former president of the EVA Clergy and the Association. She is an active member of The Suffolk Interdenominational Ministerial Alliance (SIMA) and the Suffolk Clergy United Association. And she is also a member of the EVA Leadership Academy.

Dr. Beard is the CEO of Madelene F. Beard Ministries, LLC, which serves as a platform for her books, speaking engagements, and other marketing items. She is the co-author of Words of Wisdom for the Heart and Soul, Volume III, Empowered by Visionary Cathy Staton, published in December 2023. This literary work was done in collaboration with 19 other co-authors. Dr. Beard's chapter in the latter publication is "The Call to Lead." She is also the author of her newest book, Called To Lead: Overcoming The Challenges Of Ministry In A Male-Dominated Space As A Woman Of Faith.

Dr. Beard is a recipient of the 2024 Inaugural Black Girl Magic Image Award— "Servant Leader of the Year," of which she is most humbled and grateful to Elder Latrese B. Carter, the Founder and CEO of the Black Girl Magic Alliance.

Her personal life is filled with love and family. Dr. Beard is happily married to Mr. Arnold H. Beard, Sr. Their pride and joy are their children: Savarna B. Nelson (George) and Arnold Jr. (Cheryl). The Beards are also blessed with two beloved granddaughters, Arielle Nelson and Chanta' Lassiter (Leighton), as well as three cherished great-granddaughters, Madison, Saffron, and Lily.